MULTIPLE-CHOICE & FREE-RESPONSE QUESTIONS IN PREPARATION FOR THE AP ECONOMICS EXAMINATION
(Micro and Macro)

(THIRD EDITION)

James Chasey *MA Economics*
Homewood-Flossmoor High School
Flossmoor, IL (retired)

College of Du Page

D&S MARKETING SYSTEMS, INC.
1205 38th Street Brooklyn, NY 11218
w w w . d s m a r k e t i n g . c o m

ISBN # 0-9787199-8-0

Preface

This book is designed to help students prepare for the Advanced Placement Examination in Microeconomics and Macroeconomics. Each of the examinations devised by The College Board is comprised of a 70-minute multiple-choice section containing 60 multiple-choice questions and a 60-minute free-response section with three questions. This book is organized in a similar manner, containing both multiple-choice and free-response questions. The Unit Exams in this book are designed to test the basic concepts of each unit of study, and involve multiple-choice and free-response questions. Each Unit Exam will help students identify areas of strength and weakness in their study of economics. The two sample exams at the end of the Microeconomics and Macroeconomics sections are designed to provide realistic assessments of students' knowledge of economics at the Advanced Placement level. New to the 3rd edition are actual student answers to the free response practice examination questions that have been graded using a standard AP rubric. I have included the rubric and an explanation for the grade given.

Every year the exam is different, and there is no substitute for actual classroom instruction. This book is designed to allow students to efficiently allocate their scarce resources. By reviewing those concepts they miss on these exams, they will hopefully learn more economics and perform better on the actual AP Examination in May. It is only with thoughtful instruction that students will succeed on the Advanced Placement Economics Examination. For those looking for more advice and support, I would strongly recommend the one day and week long workshops offered by the College Board.

I would like to thank my two editors, Professor David Anderson of Centre College, in Kentucky, and Tamra Carl of Hinsdale Central High School, and Illinois Virtual High School of IMSA, in Illinois. Their careful and thorough critique of my work helped make the finished product what it is. I would also like to thank the Advanced Placement Economics students at Barrington High School and their teacher, Kyle Derickson, whose input was critical in completing this edition. With all of the feedback received from colleagues and students I hope this book serves its readers well. As with all such works, any errors that remain are those of the author.

I would like to dedicate this book to all of the economics students I have had in class since 1969, especially Cara Stepanczuk. Cara was a former Advanced Placement Economics student of mine and Chasey/Sprinkel scholarship winner. She went on to earn a degree in economics at Case Western Reserve and now works at the Federal Reserve Bank. Her comments and corrections were critical to completing the 3rd edition. I would also like to dedicate this work to my two daughters, Lauren and Karen, and my wife, Julie. Lauren and Karen continue to provide me with a constant reminder that wants are unlimited and resources are scarce. Julie is glad this revision is complete and our house is now free of paperwork, for the time being.

All communications concerning this book should be addressed to:

D&S Marketing Systems, Inc.
1205 38th Street
Brooklyn, NY 11218
www.dsmarketing.com

TABLE OF CONTENTS

Microeconomics: Unit I

Scarcity and Opportunity Cost

1. The "central economic problem" results from

   (A) unlimited human wants with limited resources.
   (B) unlimited human wants with unlimited resources.
   (C) limited human wants with limited resources.
   (D) limited human wants with unlimited resources.
   (E) limitless human wants with limitless resources.

2. Attempts to deal with scarcity have included which of the following?

   (A) tradition-based resource allocation solutions
   (B) command-based resource allocation solutions
   (C) market-based resource allocation solutions
   (D) resource allocation solutions based on a mixture of the above
   (E) none of the above could be considered solutions to the scarcity problem in economics

3. The difference between "economic" and "non-economic" goods (or free goods) centers around the concept that

   (A) non-economic goods have no explicit production costs while economic goods do
   (B) non-economic goods have no implicit production costs while economic goods do
   (C) non-economic goods have no implicit or explicit production costs while economic goods do
   (D) non-economic goods have no opportunity costs while economic goods do
   (E) non-economic goods have only opportunity costs while economic goods don't

4. The "scarce resources" referred to in economics are

   I. land
   II. labor
   III. capital
   IV. money
   V. entrepreneurship

   (A) I, II, and IV
   (B) I, II, III, and IV
   (C) I, II, III, and V
   (D) II, III, IV
   (E) I, II, III, IV, and V

5. In a typical circular flow diagram there are

   I.   product markets
   II. resource markets
   III. households
   IV. businesses

   (A) I only
   (B) II only
   (C) I and II only
   (D) I, II, and III only
   (E) I, II, III, and IV

6. Production possibility curves are most often used to demonstrate

   (A) opportunity costs
   (B) dollar costs
   (C) explicit costs only
   (D) fixed costs
   (E) production costs

Questions 7 – 9 refer to the graphs below.

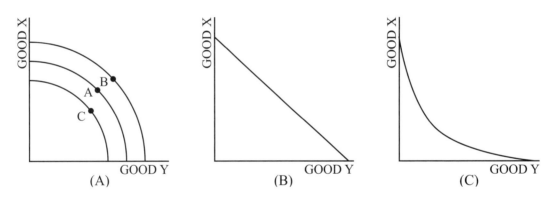

7. The production possibility curves in the graphs above demonstrate respectively

   (A) increasing opportunity cost, constant opportunity cost, decreasing opportunity cost
   (B) constant opportunity cost, increasing opportunity cost, decreasing opportunity cost
   (C) constant opportunity cost, decreasing opportunity cost, increasing opportunity cost
   (D) decreasing opportunity cost, constant opportunity cost, increasing opportunity cost
   (E) decreasing opportunity cost, increasing opportunity cost, constant opportunity cost

8. Movement from point A to point B on the production possibility curve in the graph above could be achieved by

   (A) employing all available resources
   (B) increasing consumer demand for the good in question
   (C) discovering additional resources
   (D) shifting production from good x to good y
   (E) increasing the production cost of goods x and y

9. Movement from point A to point C on the production possibility curve in the graph above could be caused by

   (A) a movement toward more free unrestricted international trade
   (B) a decrease in consumer demand for good X and good Y
   (C) a technological breakthrough that reduces production costs for all goods
   (D) lower birth rates and increased governmental regulation
   (E) lower interest rates that result in an increase in the capital stock

   _____

10. Economists would agree that

    (A) normative statements focus on facts while positive statements involve value judgments
    (B) normative statements involve value judgments while positive statements focus on facts
    (C) normative and positive statements both focus on facts and neither involve value judgments
    (D) normative and positive statements both involve value judgments and neither focus on facts
    (E) normative statements involve value judgments and focus on facts while positive statements only focus on facts

Question 11 refers to the graphs below.

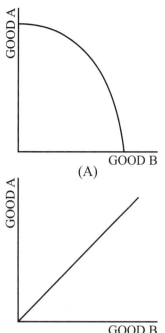

(A)

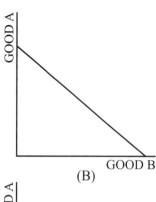

(B)

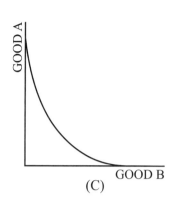

(C)

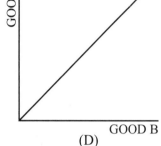

(D)

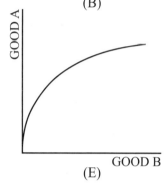

(E)

11. If the land, labor, and capital used in the production of goods A and B are very similar, then the correct shape for the production possibility curve for these two goods is best represented by which of the graphs above?

(A)   A
(B)   B
(C)   C
(D)   D
(E)   E

---

12. Markets fail to provide efficient outcomes when

(A)   positive externalities occur
(B)   negative externalities occur
(C)   perfect competition occurs
(D)   A and/or B above occur
(E)   A, B, and C above occur

Question 13 refers to the graph below.

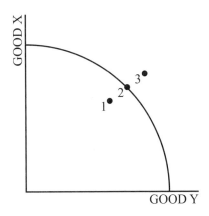

13. Points 1, 2, and 3 on the production possibility curve above best portray respectively

   (A) an efficient level of production, an unattainable level of production, and an inefficient level of production
   (B) an unattainable level of production, an efficient level of production, and an inefficient level of production
   (C) an inefficient level of production, an efficient level of production, and an unattainable level of production
   (D) an inefficient level of production, an unattainable level of production, and an efficient level of production
   (E) an efficient level of production, an inefficient level of production, and an unattainable level of production

―――――――――――

14. In a typical circular flow diagram, there are four factors of production. These four factors correctly linked with their returns are

   (A) land, labor, capital, and entrepreneurship with rent, wages, interest, and profit
   (B) land, labor, capital, and money with rent, wages, profit, and interest
   (C) labor, capital, money, and entrepreneurship with wages, profit, interest, and rent
   (D) capital, money, entrepreneurship, and factors with profit, interest, rent, and returns
   (E) money, capital, stocks, and bonds with interest, rent, dividends, and capital gain

15. Which of the following would shift a production possibility curve outward (to the right)?

   (A) an increase in consumer demand.
   (B) a decrease in consumer demand.
   (C) continued depletion of non-renewable resources.
   (D) a decrease in international trade restrictions.
   (E) a decrease in population.

<u>Questions 16 and 17</u> refer to the graph below.

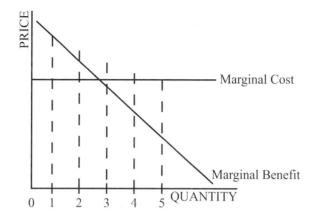

16. Based on the information in the graph above, a rational consumer would purchase how many music downloads?

    (A) 0
    (B) 1
    (C) 2
    (D) 3
    (E) 4

17. Which of the following are correctly demonstrated in the graph above?

    (A)   constant benefit
    (B)   constant cost
    (C)   diminishing cost
    (D)   diminishing opportunity cost
    (E)   a completely unrealistic portrayal of the music industry

----

18. People tend to make poor life decisions when

    (A)   costs are clear and benefits are clear
    (B)   costs are unclear and benefits are clear
    (C)   costs are unclear and benefits are unclear
    (D)   explicit costs are greater than explicit benefits
    (E)   explicit benefits are greater than explicit costs.

Questions 19 and 20 refer to the graph below.

	Country A	Country B
Corn	10	5
Computers	20	15

19. Assume that Countries A and B have identical technologies and equal amounts of resources. The table above shows outputs produced per day if the countries were to make only one good or the other. On this basis

    (A) country A has an absolute advantage in the production of corn only
    (B) country B has an absolute advantage in the production of corn only
    (C) country A has an absolute advantage in the production of corn and computers
    (D) country B has an absolute advantage in the production of corn and computers
    (E) both countries are at an equal absolute advantage

20. Based on the information in the table above

    (A) country A has a comparative advantage in the production of corn
    (B) country B has a comparative advantage in the production of corn
    (C) country A has a comparative advantage in the production of both corn and computers
    (D) country B has a comparative advantage in the production of both corn and computers
    (E) country A has a comparative advantage in the production of computers

Free-Response Questions

1. The following is a production possibility table for the production of computers and corn:

	Combination				
	I	II	III	IV	V
Computers	0	2	4	6	8
Corn	30	27	21	12	0

   (a) Demonstrate these various combinations of computers and corn graphically.
   (b) What is the significance of the points on the curve you drew in part A, as opposed to points under (or inside) the curve?
   (c) How could you use your graph to demonstrate that this economy is experiencing unemployment?
   (d) Assume that a technological breakthrough makes it possible to produce more computers with any given level of inputs. On your graph for part A, draw the new production possibility curve that would result and label it PPC- D.
   (e) Now assume that a technological breakthrough occurs that positively impacts the production of all goods. On your graph for part A, draw the new production possibility curve that would result and label it PPC-E.
   (f) Describe how your graph would look if there were a change in tastes or preferences that resulted in society demanding more computers.

2. Assume a closed, private, market economy with a business sector and a household sector

   (a) Draw and label a circular flow diagram for this economy.
   (b) On your diagram, clearly label the resource market and the product market.

3. Jim and Julie are considering whether they should go on vacation to their favorite destination. Jim argues that they cannot afford to go and Julie argues that they can afford to go. The following is a list of expected expenses for the trip. $500 each for airfare, $450 for car rental, $600 for a motel, and $375 for admission charges to events and buying memorabilia. By going on vacation, Jim will not be able to work and earn his normal hourly rate of $30 per hour for 40 hours per week. Julie works on a salary and earns $1,200 per week whether or not she is on vacation. They both eat at restaurants exclusively. Their food expenses are normally $350 per week and they estimate that their food expenses for the vacation would be the same as at home. Calculate the cost of going on vacation for Jim and Julie. Be sure to list all of the component parts of your answer.

8

Microeconomics: Unit II

The Price Discovery Mechanism

1. The various quantities of a good that producers are willing to produce at each possible price is the definition of

    (A) demand
    (B) quantity demanded
    (C) supply
    (D) quantity supplied
    (E) equilibrium

2. If the marginal utility associated with additional units of a good were constant then

    (A) the demand curve would be downward sloping
    (B) the demand curve would be upward sloping
    (C) the demand curve would be horizontal
    (D) the demand curve would be vertical
    (E) the demand curve would not exist

Question 3 refers to the graph below.

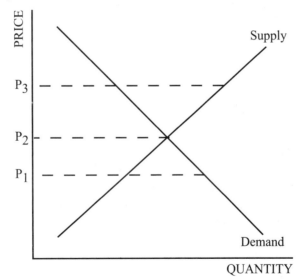

3. Using the graphs above, what is the effect of the government setting the price at P_3?

    (A) it would have no effect
    (B) it would create a surplus
    (C) it would create a shortage
    (D) it would create an equilibrium
    (E) it would create a deficit

9

4. An effective price ceiling would

   (A) be set above the equilibrium price
   (B) be set below the equilibrium price
   (C) be set at the equilibrium price
   (D) create a surplus
   (E) eliminate all consumer surplus

5. A rise in the price of peanut butter, a complementary good for jelly, will

   (A) increase the demand for jelly
   (B) increase the demand for peanut butter
   (C) decrease the demand for jelly
   (D) decrease the demand for peanut butter
   (E) decrease the price of jelly

6. A good is classified as inferior if the demand for it increases when

   (A) its price increases
   (B) its price decreases
   (C) consumers' incomes increase
   (D) consumers' incomes decrease
   (E) the price of a substitute increases

7. Which of the following is the most likely to decrease the demand for David Colander economics textbooks?

   (A) a rise in the price of David Colander textbooks
   (B) a decrease in the price of David Colander textbooks
   (C) a rise in the incomes of textbook consumers
   (D) the introduction of the new J. Charles Chasey economics textbook
   (E) news that using David Colander's text improves student scores on the AP Economics examination

8. In the absence of externalities, market prices are preferred to administered prices by economists for which of the following reasons?

   (A) market prices always result in greater consumer surplus
   (B) market prices always result in greater producer surplus
   (C) market prices always result in greater total surplus
   (D) market prices are less efficient
   (E) market prices create surplus

<u>Question 9</u> refers to the graph below.

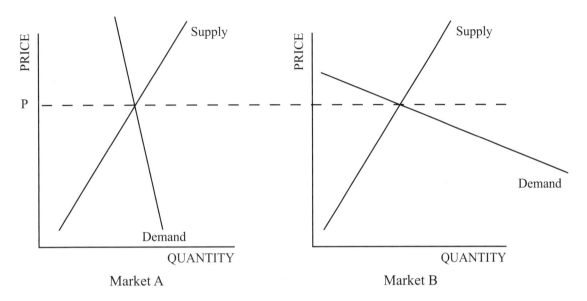

Market A   Market B

9. Based on the graphs above, if the government were to impose a per unit tax on producers, the result would be

   (A) more revenue collected by the government in Market A than in Market B
   (B) more revenue collected by the government in Market B than in Market A
   (C) a greater reduction in equilibrium quantity in Market A
   (D) a greater increase in equilibrium price in Market B
   (E) the same changes in revenue, quantity and price in both Markets

10. What will be the effect on equilibrium price and equilibrium quantity if the supply decreases and the demand increases?

   (A) price will increase, quantity will increase
   (B) price will increase, quantity will decrease
   (C) price will be indeterminate, quantity will be indeterminate
   (D) price will increase, quantity will decrease
   (E) price will increase, quantity effect will be indeterminate

11. Changes in which of the following will affect the demand for economics workbooks?

   (A) the cost of producing economics workbooks
   (B) the price of economics workbooks
   (C) expectations of future price increases in the economics workbook market
   (D) a corporate tax on economics workbooks
   (E) the price of paper changing

<u>Questions 12 and 13</u> refer to the graph below.

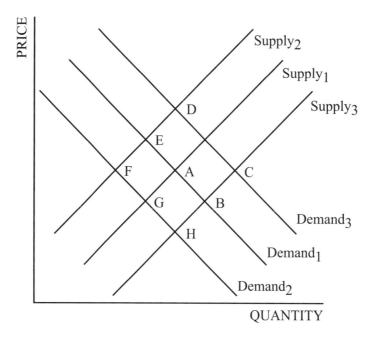

12. Using the graph above, a movement from A to B could be caused by

    (A) an increase in the price of the good
    (B) a decrease in the cost of production of the good
    (C) a decrease in the price of a substitute good
    (D) an increase in the price of a complementary good
    (E) a decrease in the number of suppliers of the good

13. Using the graph above, assuming that we begin at point A, a movement to point H could be caused by

    (A) a decrease in the price of the good
    (B) an increase in production cost and a decrease in popularity of the good
    (C) an increase in production cost and an increase in the price of a substitute good
    (D) an increase in production cost and an increase in the price of a complementary good
    (E) a decrease in production cost and an increase in the price of a complementary good

_____

Question 14 refers to the graph below.

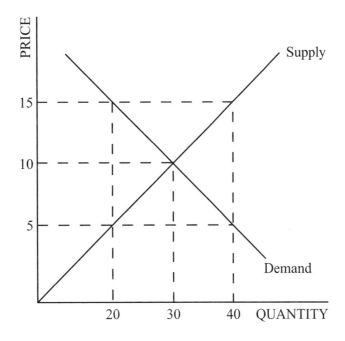

14. If the actual price in the graph above is $5, we would conclude that

    (A) a shortage of 20 exists
    (B) a shortage of 40 exists
    (C) a shortage of 10 exists
    (D) a surplus of 20 exists
    (E) a surplus of 30 exists

15. Which of the following is most likely to have a price inelastic demand?

    (A) luxuries
    (B) necessities
    (C) goods with many close substitutes
    (D) a good for which the customer has lots of time to shop
    (E) a good which constitutes an extremely large share of a buyer's budget

16. When Julie's Junque Shop put their inventory on sale they noticed that their total revenue went down. From this information we can accurately conclude that Julie is facing

    (A) inelastic demand
    (B) elastic demand
    (C) unit elastic demand
    (D) selling a normal good
    (E) selling an inferior good

<u>Question 17</u> refers to the graph below.

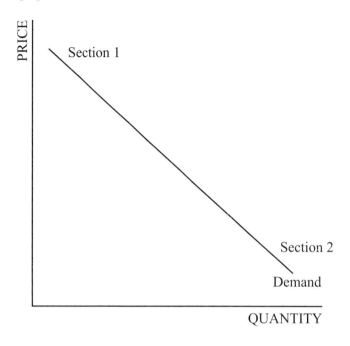

17. Using the information in the graph above, we would expect demand to be

    (A)   elastic in Section 1
    (B)   inelastic in Section 1
    (C)   unit elastic in all Sections
    (D)   inelastic in all Sections
    (E)   elastic in all Sections

---

18. Assuming the demand for illegal drugs to be very inelastic, the supply to be fairly elastic, and that one of the largest costs to society of illegal drugs is crime, which of the following would be favored by economists to lower the crime rate?

    (A)   a drug intervention program that aims enforcement at sellers
    (B)   programs focused on reducing the demand for drugs
    (C)   programs aimed at eliminating the source of illegal drugs
    (D)   lowering the penalty for those caught using illegal drugs
    (E)   raising the penalty for those caught selling illegal drugs

Questions 19 – 20 refer to the graph below.

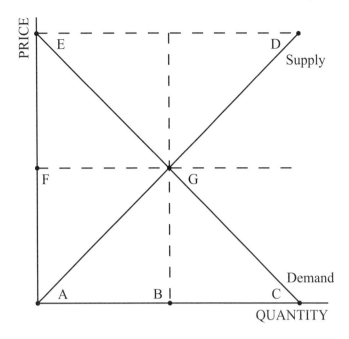

19. Using the information in the graph above, at equilibrium the consumer surplus that would result is described by the area bounded by

    (A) A, G, F
    (B) A, B, G
    (C) F, G, E
    (D) A, G, E
    (E) A, G, C

20. Using the information in the graph above, at equilibrium the producer surplus that would result is described by the area bounded by

    (A) A, G, F
    (B) A, B, G
    (C) F, G, E
    (D) A, G, E
    (E) A, G, C

21. If it is true that as consumers' incomes increase, they decrease their purchases of used clothing, then we can conclude that used clothing is

    (A) a good that validates the law of downward sloping demand
    (B) an independent good
    (C) a normal good
    (D) an inferior good
    (E) a luxury good

22. A utility maximizing consumer would allocate his or her income in such a way as to

    (A) allocate each additional dollar of income to the product that gives the highest total utility
    (B) allocate each additional dollar of income to the product that gives the highest marginal utility
    (C) allocate each additional dollar of income to the product that gives the highest marginal utility per dollar
    (D) allocate each additional dollar of income to the product that is the least expensive
    (E) not enough information is provided to make an economically valid conclusion

Questions 23 – 25 refer to the graph below.

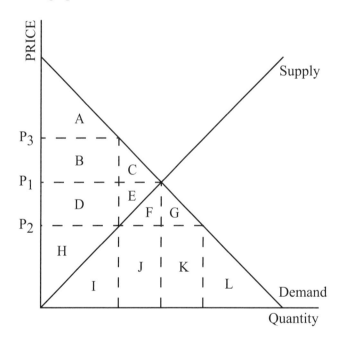

23. At a price of P_1 consumer surplus would be described by the area:

    (A) A
    (B) A & B
    (C) A, B, & C
    (D) A, B, C, D, E, & H
    (E) A – L

24. If a price of P_2 were to be administered by the government the result would be

	Consumer Surplus	Producer Surplus	Deadweight Loss
(A)	A+B+C	D+E+H	F+G
(B)	A+B+C+D+E	H	F+G
(C)	A	F+I+J	C+E
(D)	A+B+D	H	C+E
(E)	A+B+D	C+E+H	F+G

25. As a result of P_3 being administered by government we could conclude that, as compared to P_1

    (A) Consumer Surplus increases and Producer Surplus increases
    (B) Consumer Surplus decreases and Producer Surplus decreases
    (C) Consumer Surplus increases and Producer Surplus decreases
    (D) Consumer Surplus decreases and Producer Surplus increases
    (E) Consumer Surplus and Producer Surplus remain unchanged

Free-Response Questions

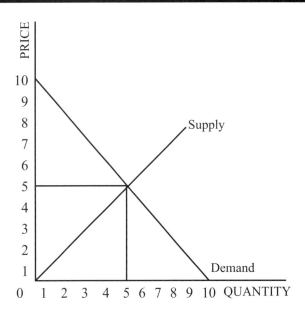

1. Assume that the graph above correctly demonstrates the supply and demand for Econ T-Shirts.

   (a)   Identify the equilibrium price and quantity of Econ T-Shirts.
   (b)   Identify the consumer surplus that results from the equilibrium price.
   (c)   Identify the producer surplus that results from the equilibrium price.
   (d)   Shade in the total surplus that results from the equilibrium price.
   (e)   Identify the new price that would result if the government imposed a binding price ceiling of $4.00 on Econ T-Shirts.
   (f)   Identify the consumer surplus that would result from the new price.
   (g)   Identify the producer surplus that would result from the new price.
   (h)   Identify the total surplus that would result from the new price.
   (i)   Compare the size of each type of surplus before and after the imposition of the price ceiling. Shade and identify by name the difference between the total surplus in part D and total surplus in part H.

18

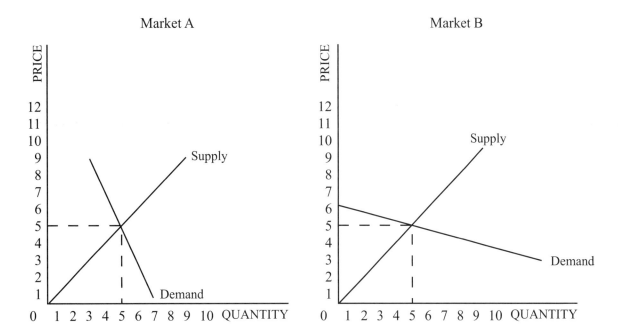

2. Market A and Market B above are two different markets for the same product. Assuming no externalities and based only on the information provided in the graphs, demonstrate on each graph the effect of a governmentally imposed tax of $2.00 on the producer of this product.

(a)   Identify the original and the new equilibrium price and quantity in Market A.

(b)   Identify the original and the new equilibrium price and quantity in Market B.

(c)   Shade in (or numerically calculate) the amount of government revenue generated by the tax in Market A.

(d)   Shade in (or numerically calculate) the amount of government revenue generated by the tax in Market B.

(e)   Identify the amount of deadweight loss due to taxation in Market A.

(f)   Identify the amount of deadweight loss due to taxation in Market B.

(g)   Identify the main difference in the way the graphs for Market A and Market B were drawn and make a conclusion with regard to the effect of the tax in each market.

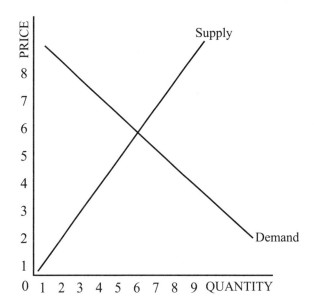

3. On the graph above, demonstrate each of the following:

   (a)   The effect of an increase in the incomes of all consumers in this market.
   (b)   The introduction into this market of an appealing substitute good with a lower price.
   (c)   A decrease in the price of a complementary good.
   (d)   The belief that in the near future this product will become less expensive.

Microeconomics: Unit III

Cost of Production & Theory of the Firm

1. Firms face certain types of costs that increase as output increases and other types of costs that are independent of output. These two costs respectively are

   (A) fixed and variable
   (B) variable and fixed
   (C) fixed and total
   (D) flexible and variable
   (E) flexible and total

Questions 2 – 4 refer to the table below.

Output	Total Revenue	Variable Cost	Fixed Cost	Total Cost
0	_____	_____	_____	100
1	_____	40	_____	_____
2	_____	60	_____	_____
3	120	75	_____	_____
4	_____	85	_____	_____
5	_____	95	_____	_____
6	_____	120	_____	_____
7	_____	200	_____	_____

2. Based on the information in the table above, the total cost of producing 6 units of output is

   (A) 100
   (B) 120
   (C) 150
   (D) 220
   (E) 240

3. Based on the information in the table above, the marginal cost of producing the 3rd unit of output is

   (A) 10
   (B) 15
   (C) 20
   (D) 75
   (E) 175

21

4. Based on the information in the table above, the price of the product this firm is selling is

   (A) $20
   (B) $40
   (C) $100
   (D) $120
   (E) not able to be determined from the information given

_____

Question 5 refers to the graphs below.

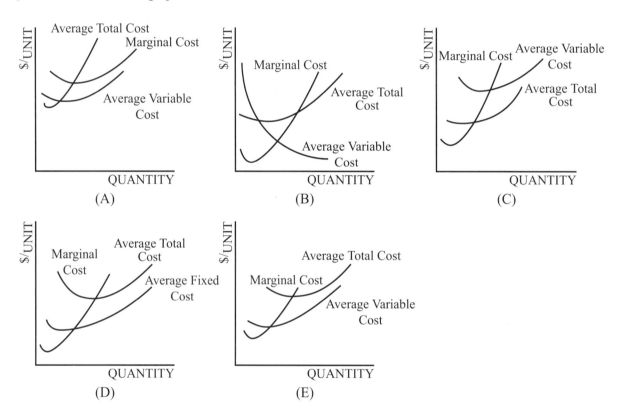

5. Which set of cost curves in the graphs above are correctly drawn?

   (A) A
   (B) B
   (C) C
   (D) D
   (E) E

_____

6. A typical marginal cost curve for a firm rises because

  (A) marginal product increases
  (B) marginal product remains constant
  (C) marginal product decreases
  (D) fixed costs rise
  (E) fixed costs fall

Question 7 refers to the graph below.

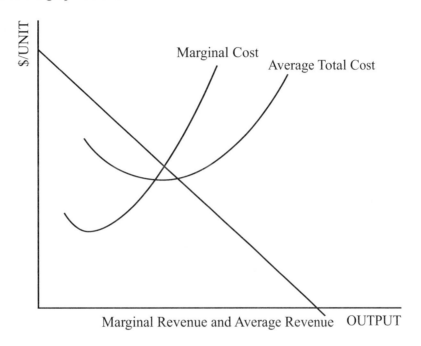

7. The firm depicted in the graph above is

  (A) a perfectly competitive firm
  (B) a perfectly price discriminating monopoly
  (C) a single price monopoly
  (D) an oligopoly in the long-run
  (E) monopolistically competitive firm in the long-run

Questions 8 and 9 refer to the table below.

Jim

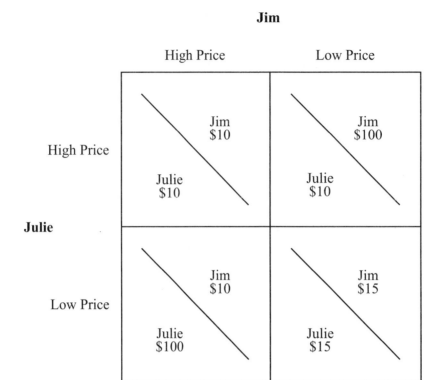

8. Based on the information in the payoff matrix box depicted above, what can be concluded?

   (A)   Jim and Julie will each charge a low price
   (B)   Jim and Julie will each charge a high price
   (C)   Jim will charge a high price and Julie will charge a low price
   (D)   Jim will charge a low price and Julie will charge a high price
   (E)   no conclusion can be accurately drawn from the information given

9. Based on the information in the payoff matrix box depicted above, what can be concluded?

   (A)   Jim has a dominant strategy and Julie does not
   (B)   Jim and Julie both have a dominant strategy
   (C)   Jim and Julie do not have a dominant strategy
   (D)   Jim does not have a dominant strategy but Julie does
   (E)   no conclusion can be accurately made from the information given in regards to dominant and
         non-dominant strategy

———————————————

10. The three basic forms of business organization are

     (A)   proprietorship, partnership, monopoly
     (B)   proprietorship, partnership, competition
     (C)   proprietorship, partnership, corporation
     (D)   proprietorship, monopoly, competition
     (E)   monopoly, competition, oligopoly

11. Firms in all market structures seek to

     (A)   maximize price and therefore maximize profit
     (B)   minimize cost and therefore maximize profit
     (C)   operate where MC = MR and are therefore guaranteed a profit
     (D)   maximize profit
     (E)   no conclusion can be accurately drawn for firms in all market structures in regard to profit maximizing behavior

12. If fixed costs for a firm operating under conditions of perfect competition increased, but not enough to lead the firm to shut down, how would that change in fixed cost affect each of the following?

	Output	Profit	Price
(A)	no change	no change	no change
(B)	no change	decrease	no change
(C)	no change	decrease	increase
(D)	decrease	decrease	increase
(E)	decrease	decrease	no change

Question 13 refers to the graph below.

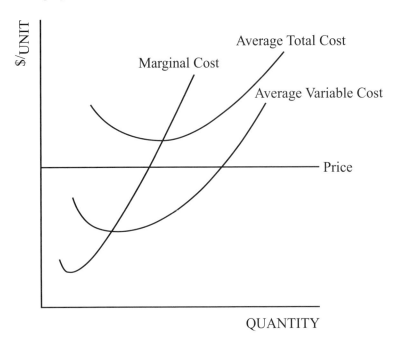

13. The graph above depicts a firm facing which combination of events?

	Profits	Entry or exit of firms to this market
(A)	positive	firms entering the market in the long run
(B)	positive	firms exiting the market in the long run
(C)	normal	firms stable in the market in the long run
(D)	negative	firms entering the market in the long run
(E)	negative	firms exiting the market in the long run

14. Marginal cost can be calculated by

    (A) adding total cost at two consecutive units of output
    (B) subtracting total cost at two consecutive units of output
    (C) adding fixed and variable cost
    (D) subtracting fixed cost from total cost
    (E) subtracting variable cost from total cost

15. Which of the following sets correctly ranks markets structures from most competitive to least competitive?

    (A) monopoly, oligopoly, monopolistic competition, perfect competition
    (B) monopoly, monopolistic competition, oligopoly, perfect competition
    (C) perfect competition, oligopoly, monopolistic competition, monopoly
    (D) perfect competition, monopoly, oligopoly, monopolistic competition
    (E) perfect competition, monopolistic competition, oligopoly, monopoly

16. Which of the following are necessary for a firm to be able to engage in price discrimination?

    I. Subdivide the market
    II. Prevent resale
    III. Monopoly power

    (A) III only
    (B) I and II only
    (C) I and III only
    (D) II and III only
    (E) I, II, and III

Question 17 refers to the graph below.

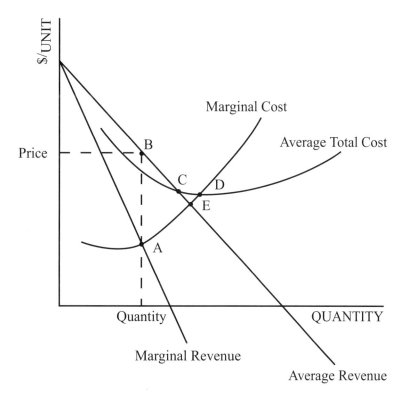

17. Based on the graph above, the monopoly price, break even price, and socially optimum price are respectively,

    (A) A, B, C
    (B) E, C, B
    (C) C, D, E
    (D) B, C, D
    (E) B, C, E

<u>Question 18</u> refers to the table below.

Figures in the table represent output.

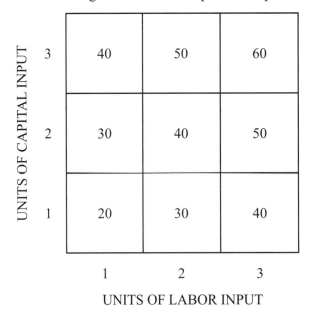

UNITS OF LABOR INPUT

18. The information in the table above is representative of a firm with

   (A)   diminishing returns to labor and constant returns to scale
   (B)   increasing returns to labor and constant returns to scale
   (C)   diminishing returns to labor and increasing returns to scale
   (D)   diminishing returns to labor decreasing returns to scale
   (E)   constant returns to labor and constant returns to scale

_____

19. Which of the following is true for both a perfect competitor and a monopolistic competitor in long-run equilibrium?

   (A)   They produce an output where they earn normal profits.
   (B)   They produce an allocatively efficient level of output.
   (C)   They produce a productively efficient level of output.
   (D)   They produce an output where MC = MR and ATC is at a minimum.
   (E)   They produce an output that is socially optimal.

Question 20 refers to the table below.

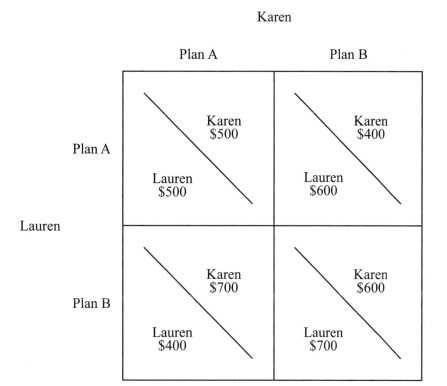

20. Which of the following is true on the basis of the table above?

    (A)   Karen has a dominant strategy but Lauren does not
    (B)   Lauren has a dominant strategy but Karen does not
    (C)   Karen and Lauren both have a dominant strategy
    (D)   neither Karen nor Lauren have a dominant strategy
    (E)   no conclusion can be made in regard to dominant strategy from the information given

Questions 21 – 23 refer to the graph below.

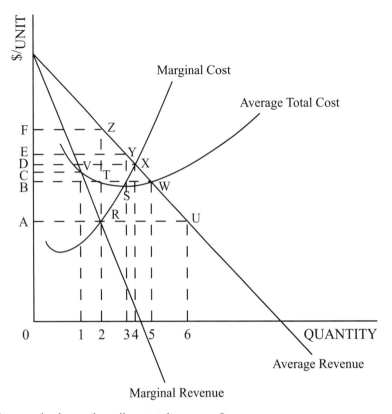

21. What area in the graph above describes total revenue?

    (A) A, R, 2, 0
    (B) F, Z, 2, 0
    (C) B, W, 5 0
    (D) D, X, 4, 0
    (E) A, U, 6, 0

22. What area in the graph above describes total cost?

    (A) A, R, 2, 0
    (B) F, Z, 2, 0
    (C) D, X, 4, 0
    (D) B, T, 2, 0
    (E) B, W, 5, 0

23. What area in the graph above represents profit or loss?

    (A) a loss of A, R, 2, 0
    (B) a profit of F, Z, 2, 0
    (C) a profit of F, Z, R, A
    (D) a loss of F, Z, T, B
    (E) a profit of F, Z, T, B

Question 24 and 25 refer to the graph below.

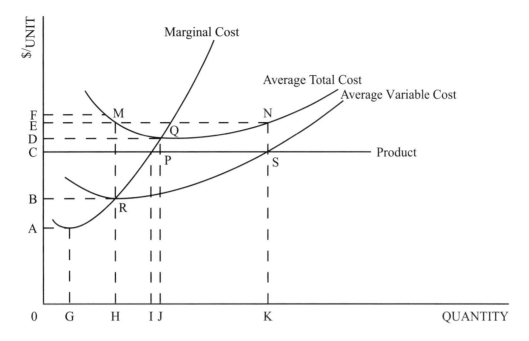

24. At what quantity in the graph above are average total costs minimized?

    (A) G
    (B) H
    (C) I
    (D) J
    (E) K

25. Based on the information in the graph above, total fixed cost is equal to

    (A) E, M, H, 0
    (B) B, R, H, 0
    (C) C, S, K, 0
    (D) D, Q, J, 0
    (E) E, N, S, C

Questions 26 – 28 refer to the graph below.

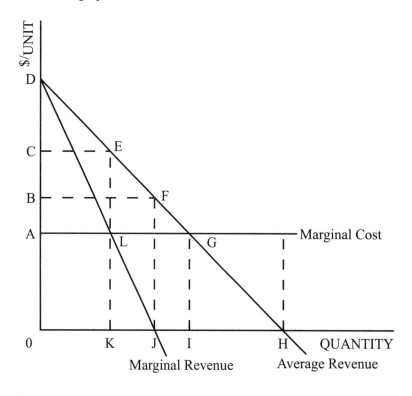

26. Based on the information in the graph above, the area of consumer surplus is represented by the area

    (A)   D, H, 0
    (B)   D, E, C
    (C)   D, J, 0
    (D)   C, E, L, A
    (E)   A, L, K, 0

27. Based on the information in the graph above, the amount of profit is represented by the area

    (A)   D, H, 0
    (B)   D, E, C
    (C)   D, J, 0
    (D)   C, E, L, A
    (E)   A, L, K, 0

28. Based on the information in the graph above, the amount of deadweight loss due to monopoly is represented by the area

    (A)   D, H, 0
    (B)   D, E, C
    (C)   D, J, 0
    (D)   E, G, L
    (E)   C, E, L, A

Question 29 and 30 refer to the graphs below.

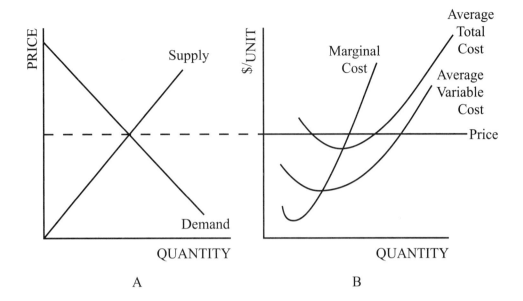

A   B

29. Based on the information in the graph above, which of the following is correct?

    (A) graph A is for the market and graph B is for the firm
    (B) graphs A and B are for the market
    (C) graphs A and B are for the firm
    (D) graph A is for the firm and graph B is for the market
    (E) graph A is for a perfectly competitive firm and graph B is for a monopoly

30. Based on the information in the graph above, which of the following is correct?

    (A) firms will enter the market and drive the price down
    (B) firms will enter the market and drive the price up
    (C) firms will exit the market and drive the price up
    (D) firms will exit the market and drive the price down
    (E) firms will neither enter not exit the market and price will remain stable

Free-Response Questions

1. Demonstrate each of the following using correctly labeled side-by-side graphs for a firm operating in long-run equilibrium in a perfectly competitive market.

    (a) If only this firm discovers a technological breakthrough that lowers the variable cost of production show what will happen to the following:
        i. the price charged by the firm
        ii. the quantity produced by the firm
        iii. the profit of the firm

    (b) Show what will happen to each of the following if, in the long run, all of the firms in the industry adopt the new technology:
        i. the price charged by the firm
        ii. the quantity produced by the firm
        iii. the profit of the firm

    Now assume that the product becomes more popular with consumers:
    (c) What will happen to the price and output in the market in the short run?
    (d) How will this affect a typical firm?
    (e) What will be the long-run effect on price and output in this market? Explain why.

2.

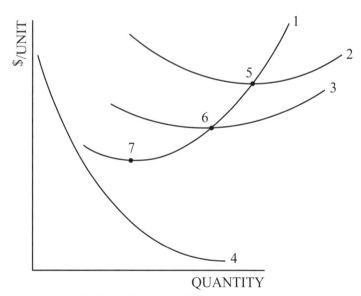

    (a) On the graph above correctly identify curves 1, 2, 3, and 4.
    (b) Identify the market structure in which this firm is operating.
    (c) If this firm is operating in a perfectly competitive market, identify a price that could exist only in short-run equilibrium.
    (d) If this firm is operating in a perfectly competitive market, identify a price that could exist only in long-run equilibrium.

34

Karen's Pricing Strategy

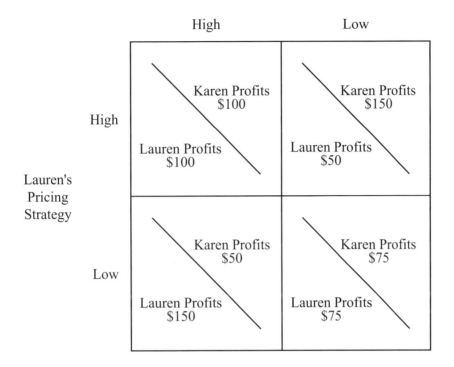

3. Karen and Lauren are two competing firms in a market where there are few competitors, selling a slightly differentiated product, with significant barriers to entry. Based on this and the information in the payoff matrix above answer each of the following:

(a) In what market structure do Karen and Lauren operate?
(b) What pricing strategy will prevail in this market? Explain how you arrived at that outcome.
(c) Does Karen have a dominant strategy? Explain.
(d) Does Lauren have a dominant strategy? Explain.
(e) If Karen and Lauren could agree to a binding, collusive agreement, what pricing strategy would prevail in this market?

Microeconomics: Unit IV

Factor Markets

Questions 1 – 3 refer to the table below.

Labor Input	Total Output
0	0
1	10
2	25
3	42
4	52
5	56
6	56
7	54

1. According to the table above, the marginal physical product of the 5th worker is

   (A) 0
   (B) 4
   (C) 11
   (D) 56
   (E) 186

2. According to the table above, diminishing returns set in with the addition of which worker?

   (A) 1
   (B) 4
   (C) 5
   (D) 6
   (E) 7

3. If the product in the figure above, sells for $10 each and workers get paid $50 per day, this company will maximize profits by hiring how many workers?

   (A) 1
   (B) 3
   (C) 4
   (D) 5
   (E) 7

Question 4 refers to the graphs below.

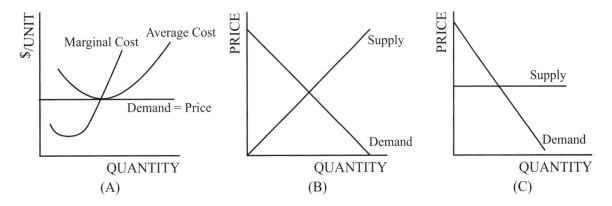

QUANTITY   QUANTITY   QUANTITY

(A)   (B)   (C)

4. In the graph's above we can conclude that graphs A and C are respectively for

    (A)   demand for the product, supply of the resource
    (B)   perfect competition, monopoly
    (C)   monopoly, perfect competition
    (D)   resource market, product market
    (E)   product market, resource market

---

5. The demand for a resource is often referred to as

    (A)   inelastic demand
    (B)   elastic demand
    (C)   unit elastic demand
    (D)   derived demand
    (E)   shifted demand

6. A rational, profit-maximizing employer would continue to hire inputs as long as

    (A)   MRP of the resource > MRC of the resource
    (B)   MRP of the resource < MRC of the resource
    (C)   price of the product > price of the resource
    (D)   price of the product < price of the resource
    (E)   MC = MR

7. The least-cost combination of resources rule is described by

    (A)   MRP = MRC
    (B)   MRPL/PL = MRCK/PK
    (C)   MPL/PL < MPK/PK
    (D)   MPL/PL = MPK/PK
    (E)   MPL/PL > MPK/PK

8. Productivity is influenced by

    I.   human capital
    II. physical capital
    III. technology

    (A) I only
    (B) II only
    (C) III only
    (D) I and II only
    (E) I, II, and III

Question 9 refers to the graph below.

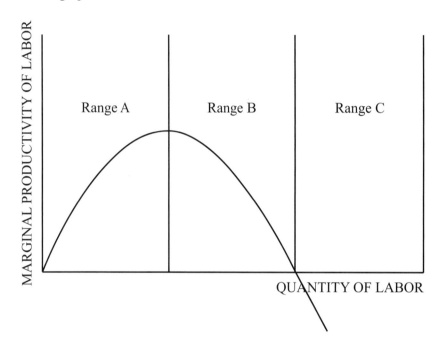

9. Ranges A, B, and C in the graph above, demonstrate respectively,

    I.   increasing marginal returns to labor
    II. diminishing marginal returns to labor
    III. constant marginal returns to labor
    IV. zero marginal returns to labor
    V.   negative marginal returns to labor

    (A) I, II, and III
    (B) I, II, and IV
    (C) I, II, and V
    (D) II, III, and IV
    (E) II, III, and V

Questions 10 and 11 refer to the table below.

Units of Labor Input	Total Product	Marginal Product	Product Price	Marginal Revenue Product
0	_____	_____	$5.00	_____
1	10	_____	$5.00	_____
2	19	_____	$5.00	_____
3	26	_____	$5.00	_____
4	31	_____	$5.00	_____
5	34	_____	$5.00	_____
6	36	_____	$5.00	_____
7	37	_____	$5.00	_____

10. Based on the information in the table above, the marginal revenue product of the 4th worker is

    (A) 5
    (B) 7
    (C) 25
    (D) 31
    (E) 37

11. Based on the information in the table above, if the product price increases from $5.00 to $7.00,

    (A) the marginal physical product will increase
    (B) the marginal physical product will decrease
    (C) the marginal revenue product will increase
    (D) the marginal revenue product will decrease
    (E) the productivity of labor will increase

12. Which of the following will increase the demand for labor?

    (A) a decrease in labor productivity
    (B) an increase in labor productivity
    (C) an increase in worker wages
    (D) a decrease in worker wages
    (E) an increase in the quantity of labor

Questions 13 and 14 refer to the graph below.

Resource A Costs $3.00 per Unit   Resource B Costs $4.00 per Unit

Quantity of Resource A	Total Product	Marginal Physical Product A	Marginal Revenue Product A	Quantity of Resource B	Total Product	Marginal Physical Product B	Marginal Revenue Product B
0				0			
1	30			1	40		
2	51			2	72		
3	89			3	96		
4	84			4	112		
5	96			5	124		
6	102			6	132		

13. Based on the information above, the least-cost-combination of Resource A and Resource B to produce 102 units of output would be

   (A)   using all of Resource A
   (B)   using all of Resource B
   (C)   using 4 units of Resource A and 1 unit of Resource B
   (D)   using 2 units of Resource A and 2 units of Resource B
   (E)   using 1 unit of Resource A and 2 units of Resource B

14. Based on the information above, which combination of resources would result in maximum profit for the firm?

   (A)   6 A and 0 B
   (B)   6 B and 0 A
   (C)   4 A and 5 B
   (D)   5 A and 4 B
   (E)   5 A and 5 B

———————————

15. If a firm can hire all of the workers it wants for $7.50 per hour and sell all of the output it can produce at a price of $5.00, we can conclude that this firm is facing

    (A)   a perfectly competitive resource market and an imperfectly competitive product market
    (B)   an imperfectly competitive resource market and an imperfectly competitive product market
    (C)   an imperfectly competitive resource market and a perfectly competitive product market
    (D)   a perfectly competitive resource market and a perfectly competitive product market
    (E)   no accurate conclusion can be made about the product market or the resources market from the information given

Free-Response Questions

1. The following table is for a perfectly competitive labor market and lists production totals for varying amounts of labor added to a fixed factory size.

Workers	Output
0	0
1	20
2	45
3	75
4	100
5	120
6	130
7	130
8	125

Answer the following questions on the basis of the information in the table above:
   (a) What is the marginal physical product of the 4th worker?
   (b) At what point (if any) does diminishing returns to labor set it?
   (c) If workers get paid $125 per day and the product that they produce sells in the market for $10 each, calculate each of the following:
      (i) The marginal revenue product for each worker
      (ii) The marginal resource cost for each worker
      (iii) The number of workers a firm in the market would employ to maximize profits

2. Assume that paper and labor are the only two inputs used in the Econville Links Factory. If the Econville Links Factory experiences a decrease in the demand for links, analyze what will happen to each of the following:

   (a) The supply and demand of Econville Links
   (b) The supply and demand for paper
   (c) The supply and demand for Links workers
   (d) Explain the process by which the change in part A affected your answer for parts B and C.

42

The price of Resource A is $2.00

The price of Resource B is $5.00

The price of the product is $3.00

Quantity of Resource A	Marginal Physical Product of Resource A	Quantity of Resource B	Marginal Physical Product of Resource B
1	10	1	40
2	9	2	30
3	8	3	25
4	7	4	20
5	6	5	15
6	5	6	10
7	4	7	5

3. On the basis of the information above answer each of the following:

   (a)   Which resource is more productive?
   (b)   What is the least-cost combination of Resource A and Resource B that this firm could use to produce 114 units of output? 142 units of output?
   (c)   What is the profit-maximizing combination of Resource A and Resource B for this firm to use?
   (d)   In what type of resource market does this firm hire its inputs? Explain.

Microeconomics: Unit V

Public Finance

Questions 1 and 2 refer to the graph below.

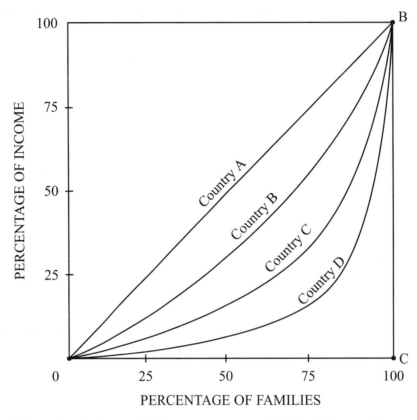

1. Based on the information in the graph above, we can conclude that this graph is a

(A) supply curve
(B) demand curve
(C) marginal cost curve
(D) Lorenz curve
(E) Coase curve

2. Using the information in the graph above, which country has the greatest degree of income inequality?

(A) A
(B) B
(C) C
(D) D
(E) they all have the same degree of income equality

3. The Gini ratio for a society in which income is distributed equally among all members would be

   (A) 0
   (B) 1
   (C) 10
   (D) 50
   (E) 100

4. A tax that is levied at a set dollar amount, like a set amount for a vehicle license, would be classified as

   (A) progressive
   (B) proportional
   (C) regressive
   (D) congressive
   (E) nominal

5. The statement: "the people who use a governmental good or service should be those who pay taxes to fund that good or service," is in agreement with the

   (A) ability-to-pay principle of taxation
   (B) ability-to-receive principle of taxation
   (C) benefits of collection
   (D) benefits-received principle of taxation
   (E) nominal vs. real principle of taxation

6. A pure public good is different than a private good in that the public good is necessarily

   (A) rival and excludable
   (B) non-rival and non-excludable
   (C) excludable
   (D) essential
   (E) important

7. In the absence of intervention, resources would be underallocated to the production of a good if

   (A) negative externalities existed
   (B) positive externalities existed
   (C) negative externalities exceeded positive externalities
   (D) neither positive or negative externalities existed
   (E) the existence of externalities does not affect resource allocation

8. Using sound economic analysis, which of the following progressively larger pollution abatement programs should be undertaken?

	Total Benefit	Total Cost
Program A.	0	0
Program B	10	3
Program C.	18	8
Program D	23	15
Program E	25	24

   (A) A
   (B) B
   (C) C
   (D) D
   (E) E

9. While relaxing at your favorite resort with the person of your dreams and having a quiet, meaningful conversation, the older group of shuffle board players begin yelling and screaming and turn up the volume on their boom-box to ear-shattering levels. The economic concept that best describes the effect of their behavior would be

   (A) consumer surplus
   (B) private goods crowding out public goods
   (C) positive externalities (or spillover benefits)
   (D) negative externalities (or spillover costs)
   (E) pure public goods

10. Which of the following comes the closest to providing an example of the "tragedy of the commons?"

   (A) ranchers over-producing cattle on their own land
   (B) hunters paying to hunt on private land
   (C) fishers catching and releasing fish on public waterways
   (D) whalers over-harvesting the open oceans of the world
   (E) sports enthusiasts paying too much for tickets to playoff games

11. A 7.5% tax on purchases at a store would be classified as

   (A) progressive and direct
   (B) proportional and direct
   (C) proportional and indirect
   (D) regressive and direct
   (E) regressive and indirect

12. The incidence of an excise tax on producers is more easily shifted to consumers

    (A) more inelastic is demand, and the more elastic is supply
    (B) more elastic is demand, and the more elastic is supply
    (C) more elastic is demand, and the more inelastic is supply
    (D) more inelastic is demand, and the more inelastic is supply
    (E) elasticities of demand and supply do not affect tax incidence

Questions 13 – 17 refer to the graph below.

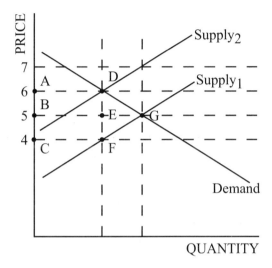

13. A tax of what size would shift the effective supply curve from $Supply_1$ to $Supply_2$ in the graph above?

    (A) $7
    (B) $6
    (C) $5
    (D) $2
    (E) $1

14. The total amount of tax paid to the government in the situation diagramed in the graph above would be the area

    (A) A, B, E, D
    (B) B, C, F, E
    (C) C, D, G, F
    (D) A, C, F, D
    (E) A, D, G, F, C

15. The amount of the total tax in the situation diagramed in the graph above paid by consumers would be

    (A) A, B, E, D
    (B) B, C, F, E
    (C) C, D, G, F
    (D) A, C, F, D
    (E) A, D, G, F, C

16. The amount of the total tax in the situation diagramed in the graph above, paid by producers would be

    (A) A, B, E, D
    (B) B, C, F, E
    (C) C, D, F, G
    (D) A, C, F, D
    (E) A, D, G, F, C

17. The deadweight loss (or efficiency loss) in the graph above, due to the tax would be

    (A) D, E, G
    (B) E, F, G
    (C) D, F, G
    (D) A, D, G, F, C
    (E) A, D, G, B

_____

18. Sources of public sector failure that could be used to argue that the public sector is inefficient in an economic sense include:

    I. special-interest effects
    II. hidden costs with clear benefits
    III. bureaucracy

    (A) I, only
    (B) II, only
    (C) III, only
    (D) I and II only
    (E) I, II, and III

Questions 19 and 20 refer to the graph below.

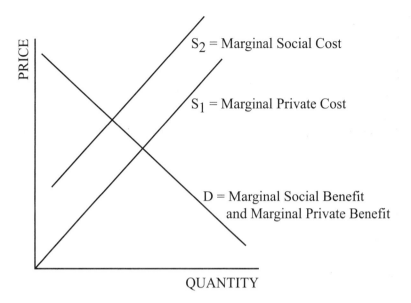

19. Based on the information in the graph above

    (A) positive externalities exist
    (B) negative externalities exist
    (C) no conclusion can be made in regard to the existence of externalities
    (D) resources are being correctly allocated to the production of this good
    (E) resources are being under-allocated to the production of this good

20. Based on the information in the graph above

    (A) taxing producers to decrease the quantity produced could correct the market failure shown and could increase efficiency
    (B) taxing producers to increase the quantity produced could correct the market failure shown and could increase efficiency
    (C) taxing producers to increase the quantity produced could correct the market failure shown and could decrease efficiency
    (D) taxing producers to decrease the quantity produced could correct the market failure shown and could decrease efficiency
    (E) taxing producers would have no effect on the quantity produced and therefore no effect on efficiency

Free-Response Questions

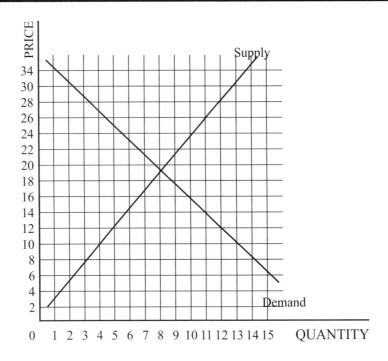

1. The supply and demand curves above are for "soon-to-be-famous" economist trading cards for James Chasey. Suppose the government of Econville, where all of these cards are sold, decides to impose a $10.00 tax per card:

   (a) Identify the new equilibrium price and quantity that will result.
   (b) Based on your graph, what conclusion can you draw about the incidence, or burden, of this newly imposed $10.00 tax?
   (c) If, for some reason, the demand for these cards were to become more inelastic, how would this affect your answers to A and B above?

2. The Pollution Abatement Board of Econville is considering a new pollution control project. Listed below are the various sizes of the project that can be undertaken. Each project is of increasing size, and the second project if undertaken would include the first. The third project if undertaken, would include the second and the first, and so on.

Project Size	Cost of the Project	Benefits of the Project
0	$0	$0
1	$10,000	$100,000
2	$40,000	$150,000
3	$90,000	$190,000
4	$160,000	$220,000
5	$260,000	$240,000

(a)   Based on the information in the table above, what would be the optimal size for the pollution control project?

(b)   Explain the reasoning process used to reach your conclusion in part A.

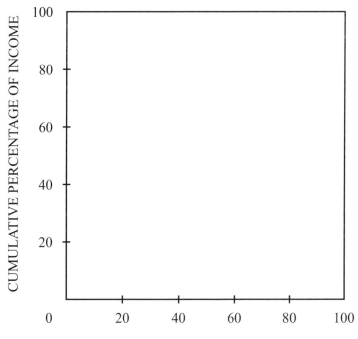

CUMULATIVE PERCENTAGE OF FAMILIES

3. Use the space provided above to do each of the following:

(a)   Draw a Lorenz curve that represents a perfectly equitable distribution of income and label it A.

(b)   Draw a Lorenz curve that represents a perfectly inequitable distribution of income and label it B.

(c)   Draw a Lorenz curve for each of the following countries and label them Country C and Country D.

Quintile	Percentage of Total Income for Country C	Percentage of Total Income for Country D
lowest 20 %	5	15
second 20 %	10	15
third 20 %	20	20
fourth 20 %	30	25
highest 20 %	35	25

(d)   Which country has a lower Gini ratio? Explain.

Microeconomics

Sample Examination I

1. A production possibilities curve will be shifted outward (to the right) by all of the following EXCEPT

   (A) a movement toward a more open free trade policy
   (B) a movement toward a more protectionist trade policy
   (C) an increase in the availability of labor
   (D) an increase in the capital stock
   (E) an increase in the general level of literacy and training of the work force

Question 2 refers to the graphs below.

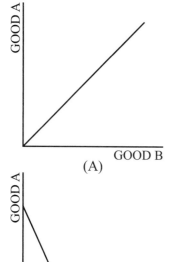
(A)

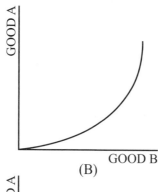
(B)

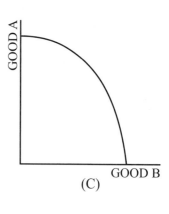
(C)

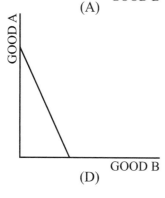
(D)

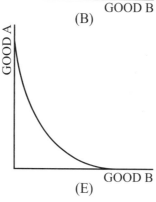
(E)

2. Which of the graphs above would be the correct one to describe the production possibilities for two goods with similar production requirements and no specialization of land, labor, and capital?

   (A) A
   (B) B
   (C) C
   (D) D
   (E) E

3. Which of the following would increase the supply of a good?

   (A) an increase in the demand for the good
   (B) a decrease in the cost of production of the good
   (C) an increase in the price of the good
   (D) a decrease in the price of the good
   (E) an increase in the price of a complementary good

4. Setting an effective price floor would

   (A) raise the actual price
   (B) lower the actual price
   (C) have no effect on the actual price
   (D) create a shortage of the good on which the floor was set
   (E) have no effect on consumer or producer surplus

5. The economic advantage that accrues to a market-based economy as compared to other systems of resource allocation is

   (A) a more equitable distribution of income
   (B) a greater ability to eliminate positive and negative externalities
   (C) a lower level of stress due to rapid technological advancement
   (D) economic efficiency
   (E) a greater sense of well being associated with slower economic change

6. Which of the following would increase the demand for a good?

   (A) an increase in the cost of production
   (B) a decrease in the price of the good
   (C) an increase in the price of the good
   (D) an increase in the price of a substitute good
   (E) an increase in the price of a complementary good

Question 7 refers to the graphs below.

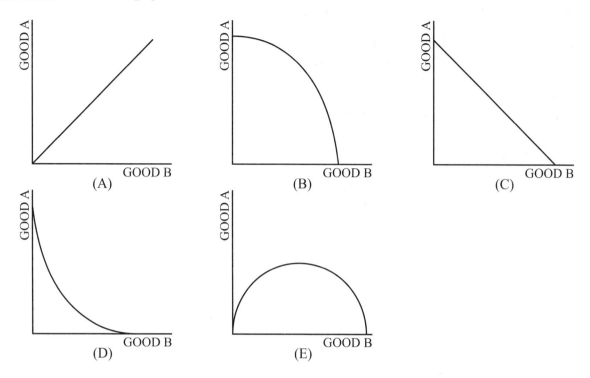

7. Which of the graphs shown above correctly demonstrates the concept of increasing opportunity cost?

(A) A
(B) B
(C) C
(D) D
(E) E

_____

8. Which of the following would decrease consumer surplus?

(A) decreasing the cost of production
(B) imposing a price ceiling
(C) an increase in supply
(D) a decrease in supply
(E) a limit on the number of producers allowed in the market

9. If a legal price floor is established on a good below the existing equilibrium price, it would

(A) raise the price of the good and raise the quantity purchased
(B) lower the price of the good and increase the quantity purchased
(C) lower the price of the good and lower the quantity purchased
(D) raise the price of the good and lower the quantity purchased
(E) have no effect on the actual price and quantity

10. The government of Econville decided to increase the user fee on its system of toll roads. This would result in the government raising more money if

    (A) the demand for the toll road is price elastic
    (B) the demand for the toll road is price inelastic
    (C) the demand for the toll road is price unit elastic
    (D) the supply of toll roads is price elastic
    (E) the supply of toll roads is price inelastic

Questions 11 – 13 refer to the figure below.

Number of workers	Output
0	0
1	7
2	15
3	24
4	27
5	29
6	29
7	28

11. The table above represents production data for a perfectly competitive firm. Based on the information in the table, the marginal physical product of the 6th worker is

    (A) 0
    (B) 5
    (C) 8
    (D) 29
    (E) 131

12. Based on the table above, the "law of diminishing returns" sets in with the addition of which worker?

    (A) first
    (B) second
    (C) fourth
    (D) sixth
    (E) seventh

13. Using the data in the table above, if workers are paid $150 and the product sells for $50, how many workers would a profit maximizing firm employ?

    (A) 0
    (B) 1
    (C) 2
    (D) 4
    (E) 7

Questions 14 – 18 refer to the graph below.

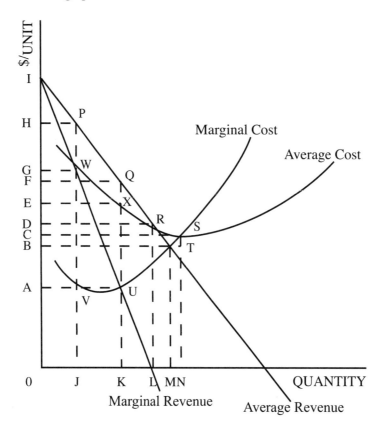

14. The Lauren and Karen Company is the sole producer of a line of fine clothing. Cost and revenue information is shown in the graph above. The Lauren and Karen Company would set the price of their clothing at level

   (A) A
   (B) C
   (C) D
   (D) F
   (E) I

15. In the graph above, the Lauren and Karen Company would maximize profits by producing a quantity of

   (A) J
   (B) K
   (C) L
   (D) M
   (E) N

16. In the graph above, the Lauren and Karen Company will have a total revenue of

    (A) OHPJ
    (B) OAUK
    (C) OAVJ
    (D) OCSN
    (E) OFQK

17. In the graph above, the Lauren and Karen Company will have a total cost of

    (A) OHPJ
    (B) OCSN
    (C) ODRL
    (D) OEXK
    (E) AFQU

18. In the graph above, the Lauren and Karen Company will earn a profit of

    (A) EFQX
    (B) GHPW
    (C) AFQU
    (D) OAUK
    (E) OCSN

Questions 19 – 20 refer to the figure below.

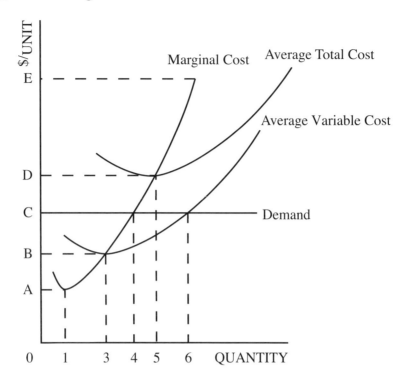

19. The situation in the graph above shows a firm in

    (A) a perfectly competitive market experiencing economic profits
    (B) a perfectly competitive market experiencing economic losses
    (C) a perfectly competitive market breaking even
    (D) an imperfectly competitive market experiencing economic profit
    (E) an imperfectly competitive market experiencing economic losses

20. The firm shown in the graph above, would shut down in the short run if the price fell below

    (A) A
    (B) B
    (C) C
    (D) D
    (E) E

_____

21. The profit maximizing rule for all firms, regardless of market structure is

    (A) AR = AC
    (B) TR = TC
    (C) P = minimum ATC
    (D) MR = MC
    (E) P = MC

22. If supply and demand both increase, we can correctly conclude that

    I. equilibrium price will rise
    II. equilibrium price will fall
    III. equilibrium price is indeterminate
    IV. equilibrium quantity is indeterminate
    V. equilibrium quantity will rise

    (A) I, only
    (B) I and V, only
    (C) II and IV, only
    (D) III and IV, only
    (E) III and V, only

23. The rule that a rational consumer would follow in deciding how to spend money when shopping for two goods, to maximize satisfaction, is expressed in which of the following?

    (A) $MR = MC$
    (B) $MU_A/P_A = MU_B/P_B$
    (C) $MRP_A/P_A = MRP_B/P_B$
    (D) Supply of A = Demand for A
    (E) Demand for A = Demand for B

24. The supply curve for a perfectly competitive firm is

    (A) equal to the falling and rising sections of the marginal cost curve
    (B) equal to the rising part of the marginal cost curve above average total cost
    (C) equal to the rising part of the marginal cost curve above average variable cost
    (D) equal to the rising part of the average total cost curve
    (E) equal to the rising part of the average variable cost curve

25. If a nation wishes to have a more equitable distribution of income, they could adopt a

    (A) higher flat rate tax
    (B) tax system based more on consumption taxes
    (C) more progressive tax system
    (D) more proportional tax system
    (E) more regressive tax system

Questions 26 – 27 refer to the figure below.

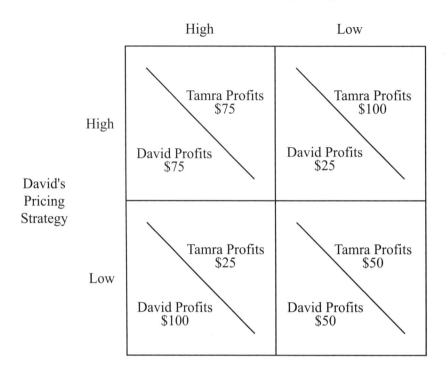

26. Based on the information in the figure above

    (A)   Dave has a dominate strategy and Tamra does not
    (B)   Tamra has a dominate strategy and Dave does not
    (C)   neither Dave nor Tamra have a dominate strategy
    (D)   both Dave and Tamra have a dominate strategy
    (E)   no conclusion can be accurately made about strategic decision making based on the information
          in the figure above

27. Based on the information in the figure above

    (A)   Tamra and Dave will both pursue a high price strategy
    (B)   Tamra and Dave will both pursue a low price strategy
    (C)   Tamra will pursue a high price strategy while Dave will pursue a low price strategy
    (D)   Dave will pursue a high price strategy while Tamra will pursue a low price strategy
    (E)   no accurate conclusion can be made about pricing strategy from the information given

Question 28 refers to the graphs below.

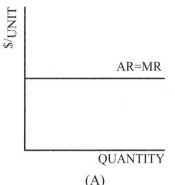

(A)

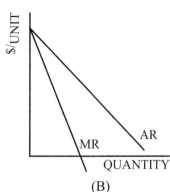

(B)

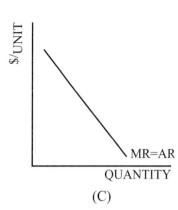

(C)

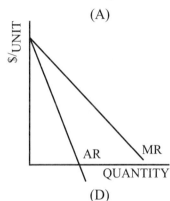

(D)

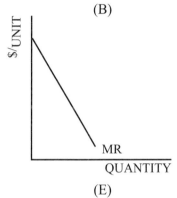

(E)

28. Which of the graphs above correctly shows the demand and marginal revenue facing a price discriminating monopolist?

    (A) A
    (B) B
    (C) C
    (D) D
    (E) E

29. Julie can chop 5 cords of wood per day or wash 12 windows. Jim can chop 1 cord of wood per day or wash 11 windows. Based only on this information

    (A) Julie has an absolute advantage in both chopping wood and washing windows.
    (B) Jim has an absolute advantage in both chopping wood and washing windows.
    (C) Julie has a comparative advantage in washing windows and Jim has a comparative advantage in chopping wood.
    (D) Julie has a comparative advantage in both washing windows and chopping wood.
    (E) Jim has a comparative advantage in both washing windows and chopping wood.

30. If producing a good creates benefits that accrue to neither the consumer nor the producer of the good, we can accurately conclude that

    (A) the market is efficient and correctly allocates resources
    (B) the market is inefficient and will over allocate resources to the production of that good
    (C) the market is inefficient and will under allocate resources to the production of that good
    (D) the market is efficient, but will over allocate resources to the production of that good
    (E) the market is efficient, but will under allocate resources to the production of that good

31. Which of the following would definitely lower the equilibrium price of a good?

    (A) increased raw materials cost and increased popularity of the product
    (B) increased raw materials cost and decreased popularity of the product
    (C) more producers and fewer consumers
    (D) fewer producers and more consumers
    (E) more producers and an increase in the price of a substitute good

32. If your insurance company increases that annual premium for your liability insurance, which of the following combinations correctly describes the effect of this on your business?

	Average Total Cost	Average Variable Cost	Marginal Cost
(A)	No Change	No Change	No Change
(B)	Increase	Increase	No Change
(C)	Increase	No Change	No Change
(D)	Increase	Increase	Increase
(E)	No Change	Increase	Increase

33. Which of the following is the best example of a pure public good?

    (A) a consumer purchasing a new car
    (B) a business purchasing a new computer
    (C) the federal government buying new submarines
    (D) a village government installing new street lights
    (E) a student paying tuition to a private school

34. If a single firm in a perfectly competitive industry develops a production technique that results in only that firm lowering its cost of production, which of the following will result for that firm?

	Price	Quantity	Profit
(A)	decrease	decrease	decrease
(B)	decrease	increase	increase
(C)	no change	decrease	increase
(D)	no change	increase	increase
(E)	increase	increase	increase

35. A business would continue to hire new workers as long as which of the following conditions is satisfied?

    (A)   MR = MC
    (B)   MRP > MRC
    (C)   MRP < MRC
    (D) $MPP_L = MPP_K$
    (E) $MPP_L/P_L = MPP_K/P_K$

36. If the demand for a product is price elastic and a government imposes an excise tax on that product, relative to the situation with an inelastic demand curve, which of the following is most likely to result?

    (A)   a relatively large decrease in use and a relatively large increase in government revenue
    (B)   a relatively large decrease in use and a relatively small increase in government revenue
    (C)   a relatively small decrease in use and a relatively large increase in government revenue
    (D)   a relatively small decrease in use and a relatively small increase in government revenue
    (E)   a relatively large increase in use and a relatively large decrease in government revenue

37. In the resource (or factor) market, what would be the most likely result of an increase in worker productivity and at the same time a decrease in the price of the product?

    (A)   an increase in the demand for labor
    (B)   a decrease in the demand for labor
    (C)   an increase in the demand for labor and the supply of labor
    (D)   a decrease in the supply of labor
    (E)   an indeterminate effect on the demand for labor

38. Perfect competitors are said to be efficient because for them, unlike for monopolies

    (A)   P > MC
    (B)   P = MC
    (C)   P < MC
    (D)   MR = MC
    (E)   MR > MC

39. If an increase in the price of one good increases the demand for another good, then these two goods are

    (A)   normal goods
    (B)   inferior goods
    (C)   public goods
    (D)   complementary goods
    (E)   substitute goods

Questions 40 – 41 refer to the graphs below.

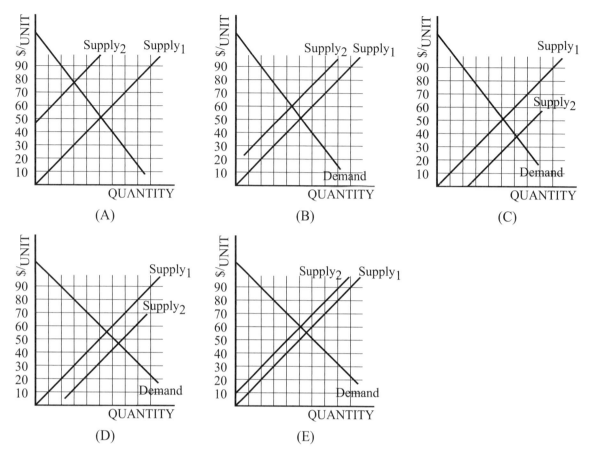

40. Which graph above correctly demonstrates the effect of the government imposing a $10 tax on the production of this good?

    (A) A
    (B) B
    (C) C
    (D) D
    (E) E

41. Based on the information in the graph above, which of the following is correct?

    (A) consumers would pay most of the tax
    (B) producers would pay most of the tax
    (C) consumers and producers would share equally in paying the tax
    (D) the equilibrium price would increase by more than the tax
    (E) the government would pay the tax

42. If two competing firms are jointly concerned about the pricing strategy of the other firm in determining their own profit maximizing price and output decision, they are mostly likely competing in which of the following markets?

    (A) perfect competition
    (B) monopolistic competition
    (C) oligopoly
    (D) single price monopoly
    (E) price discriminating monopoly

43. A $10 tax levied on each resident of a community would be considered a

    (A) progressive tax
    (B) proportional tax
    (C) regressive tax
    (D) Laffer tax
    (E) marginal tax

44. If Lauren's Laundry experiences an increase in rent and insurance, what will be the effect on production costs?

    (A) only fixed cost will increase
    (B) only marginal cost will increase
    (C) only variable cost will increase
    (D) marginal cost and total cost will increase
    (E) total cost and fixed cost will increase

Question 45 refers to the table below.

Labor

	0	1	2	3
1		100	200	300
2		200	300	400
3		300	400	500

Capital

Figures in the table represent output.

45. The numbers in the table above are for a firm that has a production process characterized by

    (A) decreasing returns to labor
    (B) constant returns to labor
    (C) increasing returns to labor
    (D) increasing returns to capital
    (E) constant returns to scale

46. A minimum wage law is an example of a(n):

    (A)   price ceiling
    (B)   price floor
    (C)   equilibrium price
    (D)   elastic supply of labor
    (E)   derived demand for labor

Questions 47 – 50 refer to the figure below.

Quantity of Output	Variable Cost	Fixed Cost	Total Cost
0	___	___	100
1	20	___	___
2	50	___	___
3	90	___	___
4	150	___	___
5	240	___	___

47. Refer to the table above. The average variable cost of producing the 3rd unit is

    (A)   30
    (B)   40
    (C)   50
    (D)   90
    (E)   100

48. Refer to the table above. The marginal cost of producing the 4th unit is

    (A)   0
    (B)   20
    (C)   60
    (D)   70
    (E)   100

49. Refer to the table above. If product price is $75.00, to maximize profits this firm will produce

    (A)   zero, the firm will lose money by producing any level of output
    (B)   zero in the short run, but 3 in the long run
    (C)   zero in the long run, but 3 in the short run
    (D)   4 in the short run, and 5 in the long run
    (E)   4 in the long run, and 4 in the short run

50. Refer to the table above. If the product price decreases to $50.00 what will this firm do?

   (A) produce in the short run but not the long run
   (B) produce in the long run but not the short run
   (C) produce in both the long run and the short run
   (D) produce in neither the long run nor the short run
   (E) shut-down in the short run but produce in the long run

---

51. A price discriminating monopolist has a price

   (A) equal to its marginal revenue
   (B) greater than its marginal revenue
   (C) less than its marginal revenue
   (D) greater than marginal cost
   (E) less than marginal cost

Question 52 refers to the graph below.

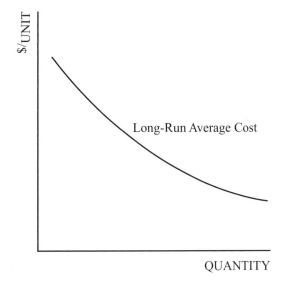

52. The Long-Run Average Cost curve in the graph above demonstrates

   (A) economies of scale
   (B) diseconomies of scale
   (C) constant returns to scale
   (D) opportunity cost
   (E) diminishing returns

Question 53 refers to the table below.

The following information is for ECON T-Shirts

Income of ECON T-Shirt Consumers	Quantity Demanded of ECON T-Shirts
$50,000	100
75,000	200
100,000	300
125,000	400
250,000	500

53. Based on the information in the table above, ECON T-Shirts are:

    (A) normal goods
    (B) inferior goods
    (C) superior goods
    (D) positive goods
    (E) negative goods

---

54. If natural disasters, such as floods, hurricanes, and tornadoes, disrupt the transportation and production of crude oil, then we can expect the

    (A) industry supply curve for gasoline to shift to the right and gasoline prices to rise
    (B) industry supply curve for gasoline to shift to the left and gasoline prices to fall
    (C) industry supply curve for gasoline to shift to the left and gasoline prices to rise
    (D) industry demand curve for gasoline to shift to the left and gasoline prices to fall
    (E) demand for gasoline to rise and gasoline prices to rise

Question 55 refers to the graph below.

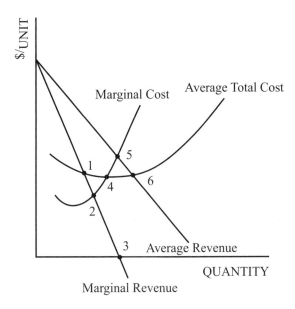

55. Based on the graph above, which of the following combinations are correct?

	Allocatively efficient point	Productively efficient point	Break-even point
(A)	1	2	4
(B)	4	5	6
(C)	1	4	6
(D)	2	4	5
(E)	5	4	6

56. Which of the following is true for a monopolistic competitor in long-run equilibrium?

(A) economic profits
(B) economic losses
(C) break even
(D) price = marginal cost
(E) price = minimum average total cost

Questions 57 – 58 refer to the graph below.

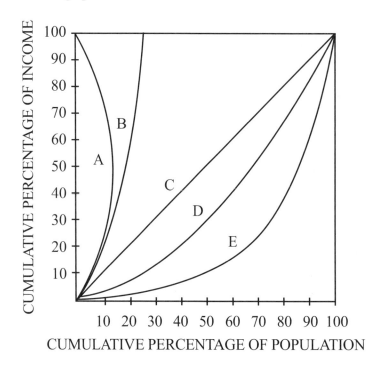

57. The graph above is a(n)

   (A)   Lorenz curve
   (B)   Laffer curve
   (C)   production possibilities curve
   (D)   marginal revenue product curve
   (E)   efficiency loss curve

58. Using the information in the graph above, the most inequitable distribution of income is demonstrated on curve

   (A)   A
   (B)   B
   (C)   C
   (D)   D
   (E)   E

59. A single-price monopolist and a price discriminating monopolist have which of the following in common?

    (A) size of consumer surplus
    (B) size of producer surplus
    (C) amount of profit
    (D) operating at where price = marginal cost
    (E) operating where marginal cost = marginal revenue

60. A firm wishing to use the least-cost combination of labor and land to produce a given output would be guided by which of the following?

    (A) marginal product of labor/price of labor = marginal product of land/price of land
    (B) marginal revenue product of labor/price of labor = marginal revenue product of land/ price of land
    (C) marginal revenue of labor/price of labor = marginal cost of land/ price of lan
    (D) marginal revenue product = marginal resource cost
    (E) marginal revenue product/price = marginal resource cost/price

Free-Response Questions

1. ChaseCo. is a firm operating in a perfectly competitive market that is at long-run equilibrium. For this constant-cost industry:

   (a) Draw a correctly labeled graph for a representative firm demonstrating the long run-equilibrium.
       (i) On your graph identify the price that ChaseCo. will charge.
       (ii) On your graph identify the quantity that ChaseCo. will produce.
   (b) Draw a correctly labeled graph for the industry next to the firm graph you drew in A.
       (i) On your graph identify the price and output for this industry.
   (c) Suppose there is a significant increase in the popularity of the product being sold in this market. Demonstrate graphically each of the following:
       (i) The short-run effect on the market price and output.
       (ii) The short-run effect on price, output, and profit for ChaseCo.
   (d) Explain what will happen to ChaseCo. and the industry in the long run.

72

2. Identify each of the following using the letters and numbers in the graph below.

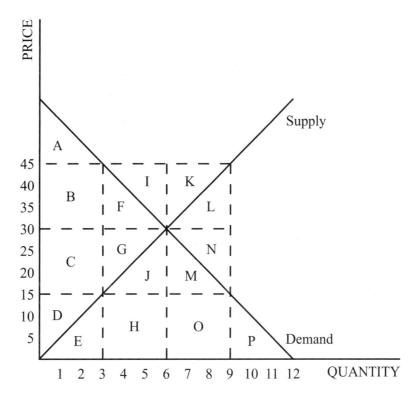

(a)   Consumer surplus
(b)   Producer surplus
(c)   Total surplus
(d)   Now assume that the government imposes an effective price ceiling. Would that price ceiling be more appropriate at $15 or $45? Explain.
(e)   Using the number and letters in the figure above, identify each of the following in the presence of the effective price ceiling you explained in part (d)
      (i)   New consumer surplus
      (ii)   New producer surplus
      (iii)   New total surplus

3. The following is a production function for the JimmyJul company. The JimmyJul company can hire all of the workers it wants for $100 per day and can sell all it can produce for $25 each.

Number of workers	Output per day
0	0
1	5
2	12
3	20
4	25
5	27
6	27
7	25

(a)   Calculate the marginal physical product of the 4th worker.
(b)   Calculate the marginal revenue product of the 5th worker.
(c)   Calculate the marginal revenue facing JimmyJul.
(d)   At what point (if any) does the law of diminishing returns set in? Explain.
(e)   Calculate the profit-maximizing number of workers for the JimmyJul company to hire.
(f)   In what type of market does JimmyJul hire its workers? Explain.
(g)   In what type of market does JimmyJul sell its output? Explain.

Microeconomics

Sample Examination II

Question 1 refers to the graph below.

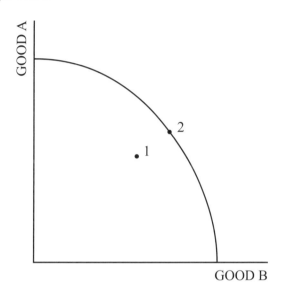

1. Movement from point 1 to point 2 on the production possibilites curve shown in the graph above could be caused by which of the following?

    (A) an increase in consumer demand
    (B) an increase in production cost
    (C) a decrease in unemployment
    (D) an increase in unemployment
    (E) a change in consumer preferences for GOOD A and GOOD B

    _____

2. The concept of derived demand is demonstrated by which of the following?

    (A) demand creates its own supply
    (B) supply creates its own demand
    (C) the demand for a product is determined by the demand for the resource
    (D) the demand for a resource is determined by the demand for the product
    (E) the supply of a resource is determined by the supply of the product

3. Setting a price floor above equilibrium would

    (A)   create a surplus of the good
    (B)   create a shortage of the good
    (C)   create an equilibrium situation of the good
    (D)   lower the actual price
    (E)   have no effect on the actual price

4. If consumers voluntarily wait for hours in line to obtain a good, but enjoy an extremely low price for that good when they get it, you could conclude that

    (A)   a market solution to resource allocation is not in effect
    (B)   there are negative externalities present
    (C)   there are positive externalities present
    (D)   the good in question is a normal good
    (E)   the good in question is an inferior good

5. A business would continue to hire additional workers as long as which of the following conditions is satisfied?

    (A) $MR = MC$
    (B) $MRP > MRC$
    (C) $MRP < MRC$
    (D) $MPP/L > MPP/K$
    (E) $MPP_L/P_L > MPP_K/P_K$

Question 6 refers to the graphs below.

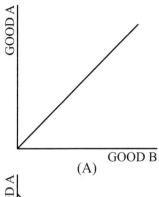

(A)

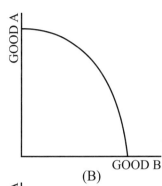

(B)

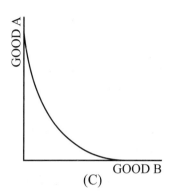

(C)

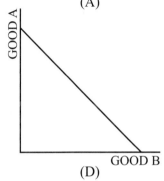

(D)

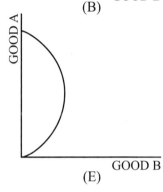

(E)

6. Which of the graphs shown above demonstrates the correct shape of a production possibilities curve for two goods with land, labor, and capital requirements that involve no specialization?

   (A) A
   (B) B
   (C) C
   (D) D
   (E) E

Questions 7 – 9 refer to the graph below.

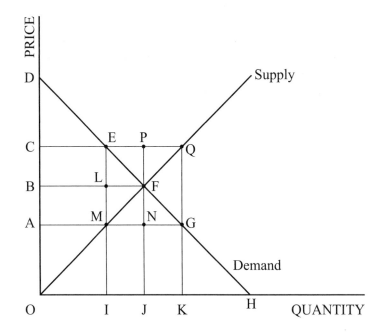

7. Based on the information in the graph above, the consumer surplus that would result from a competitive equilibrium would be represented by the area

   (A) ODF
   (B) ODH
   (C) OBF
   (D) MEF
   (E) BDF

8. Using the information in the graph above, the result of an effective price ceiling set at A would be

   (A) shortage of K - I
   (B) shortage of I - O
   (C) shortage of J - I
   (D) surplus of J – I
   (E) surplus of I - O

9. Using the information in the graph above, the efficiency loss that would result from a price ceiling set at A would be

   (A) ODF
   (B) OBF
   (C) MEF
   (D) MFG
   (E) EFQ

10. The government of Econville has decided to engage in a stop smoking campaign for its residents. Which of the following would be most effective in accomplishing that goal?

    (A) tax cigarettes, as their demand is elastic and such a tax would discourage use
    (B) tax cigarettes, as their demand is price inelastic and such a tax would discourage their use
    (C) develop a smoker education program to decrease the demand for cigarettes; since their demand is price inelastic and a tax plan will not be an effective deterrent
    (D) develop a smoker education program to decrease the demand for cigarettes; since their demand is price elastic a tax plan will not be an effective deterrent
    (E) set a price ceiling to discourage use by smokers

Questions 11 – 13 refer to the table below.

Number of workers	Output
0	0
1	10
2	25
3	45
4	60
5	70
6	70
7	60

11. The table above represents production data for a perfectly competitive firm. Based on the information in the table, the marginal physical product of the 7th worker is

    (A) -10
    (B) 0
    (C) 10
    (D) 60
    (E) 340

12. In the table above, the "law of diminishing returns" sets in with the addition of which worker?

    (A) First
    (B) Second
    (C) Fourth
    (D) Sixth
    (E) Seventh

13. Using the data in the table above, if workers are paid $250 and the product being produced sells for $20, how many workers would a profit maximizing firm employ?

    (A) 3
    (B) 4
    (C) 5
    (D) 6
    (E) 7

Questions 14 – 17 refer to the table below.

Quantity of Output	Average Variable Cost	Average Fixed Cost	Average Total Cost
0	___	___	___
1	30	200	___
2	25	___	___
3	30	___	___
4	40	___	___
5	50	___	___
6	60	___	___

14. The total cost of producing 4 units is

    (A) 40
    (B) 50
    (C) 90
    (D) 260
    (E) 360

15. The marginal cost of producing the 5th unit is

    (A) 40
    (B) 70
    (C) 90
    (D) 360
    (E) 450

16. If product price is $35, to maximize profits this firm will produce

    (A) zero, the firm will lose money by producing any level of output
    (B) zero in the short run, but 2 in the long run
    (C) zero in the long run, but 2 in the short run
    (D) 3 in the short run, and 4 in the long run
    (E) 3 in the long run, and 5 in the short run

17. Refer to the table above. If the product price increases to $100.00 what will this firm do?

(A) produce in the short run but not the long run
(B) produce in the long run but not the short run
(C) produce in both the long run and the short run
(D) not produce in either the long run or the short run
(E) shut down in the short run but produce in the long run

Questions 18 – 22 refer to the figure below.

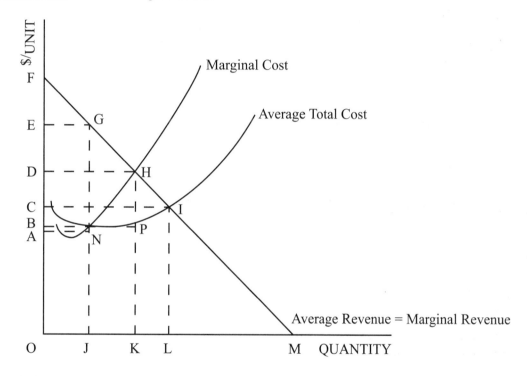

18. The Jimbo Company has cost and revenue data as diagramed in the graph above. Based on this information the Jimbo Company is a

(A) perfect competitor in long run equilibrium
(B) perfect competitor in short run equilibrium
(C) price discriminating monopolist
(D) single price monopolist
(E) monopolistic competitor in long run equilibrium

19. In the graph above, the Jimbo Company will maximize profits by producing a quantity of

(A) O
(B) M
(C) J
(D) K
(E) L

20. In the graph above, the Jimbo Company will have a total revenue of

    (A) OANJ
    (B) OFHK
    (C) OFM
    (D) OCIL
    (E) ODHK

21. In the graph above, the Jimbo Company will have a total cost of

    (A) OBPK
    (B) OANJ
    (C) OEGJ
    (D) OBPK
    (E) OCIL

22. In the graph above, the Jimbo Company will earn a profit of

    (A) OANJ
    (B) BFHP
    (C) OEGJ
    (D) OCIL
    (E) ODHK

---

23. To an economist, the real cost of taking this test, includes all of the following EXCEPT

    (A)   the enjoyment from attending a concert at the time of this test
    (B)   the money you could have earned from work during this test
    (C)   the price you paid to enroll in the class giving this test
    (D)   the fatigue you will certainly suffer from taking this test
    (E)   the knowledge you will gain from taking this test

Questions 24 – 25 refer to the graphs below.

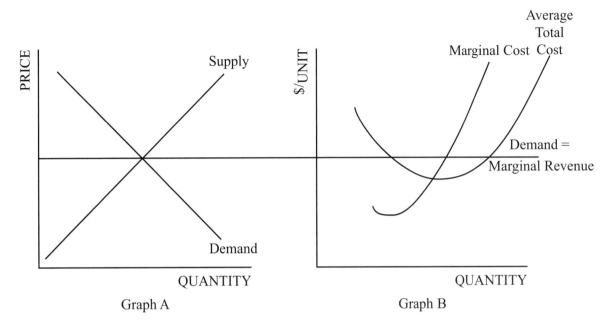

Graph A   Graph B

24. The situation in the graphs above shows

    (A)   a market in Graph A and a firm earning economic profits in Graph B
    (B)   a market in Graph A and a firm breaking even in Graph B
    (C)   a market in Graph A and a firm earning economic losses in Graph B
    (D)   a firm in Graph A and a market in long run equilibrium in Graph B
    (E)   a firm in Graph A and a market in short run equilibrium in Graph B

25. The firm shown in the graph above is a(n)

    (A)   perfect competitor
    (B)   monopolistic competitor
    (C)   oligopoly
    (D)   single-price monopolist
    (E)   price-discriminating monopolist

26. If supply increases and demand decreases, we can correctly conclude that

    I. equilibrium price will rise
    II. equilibrium price will fall
    III. equilibrium price is indeterminate
    IV. equilibrium quantity is indeterminate
    V. equilibrium quantity will rise

    (A) I only
    (B) I and IV only
    (C) II and IV only
    (D) III and IV only
    (E) III and V only

27. Which of the following is not recognized as a limitation of the market system?

    (A) market failure
    (B) failure of market outcomes
    (C) positive externalities
    (D) negative externalities
    (E) efficiency

28. A market supply curve for a perfectly competitive industry is

    (A) the horizontal sum of the individual firms' supply curves
    (B) the same as the individual firm's supply curve
    (C) the rising part of a firm's marginal cost curve above its variable cost
    (D) the sum of the equilibrium prices and quantities for all firms in the market
    (E) the sum of consumer and producer surplus

29. A nation would move toward a more equitable distribution of income if they adopted a tax system of

    (A) flat rate taxes
    (B) consumption based taxes
    (C) progressive taxes
    (D) proportional taxes
    (E) regressive taxes

Question 8 refers to the graphs below.

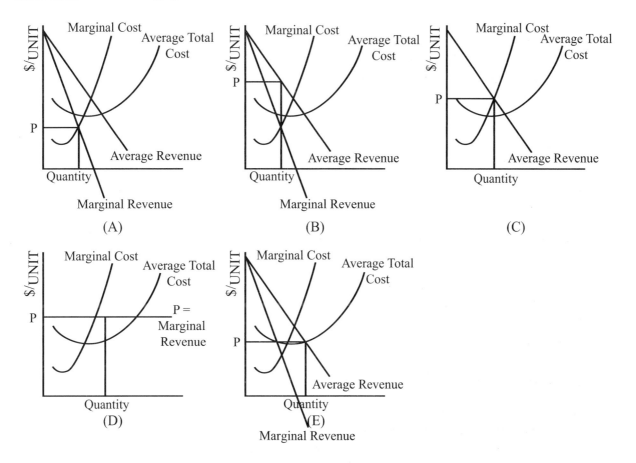

30. Which of the graphs above correctly shows the profit-maximizing price and output for a single-price monopolist?

    (A) A
    (B) B
    (C) C
    (D) D
    (E) E

31. As used in economics, the term economic rent means

    (A) a monthly payment for an apartment
    (B) the return for land
    (C) monetary payment of a royalty
    (D) a return to a factor of production above the minimum payment necessary to employ that resource
    (E) an inefficient output level

32. All forms of imperfect competition are considered to be inefficient because they operate at a point where

    (A) P > MC
    (B) P = MC
    (C) P < MC
    (D) P > MR
    (E) P = MR

33. In which market structure are there, few firms competing, significant barriers to entry, and interdependent pricing and output decisions?

    (A) perfect competition
    (B) monopolistic competition
    (C) oligopoly
    (D) single price monopolist
    (E) price discriminating monopolist

34. If the company that supplies the raw materials for your production process increases the price they charge and the fuel to run your machines in that production process also increases in price, which of the following combinations correctly describes the effect of this on your business?

	Average Total Cost	Average Variable Cost	Marginal Cost
(A)	No Change	No Change	No Change
(B)	Increase	Increase	No Change
(C)	Increase	No Change	No Change
(D)	Increase	Increase	Increase
(E)	No Change	Increase	Increase

35. If business people adopt a relatively positive attitude about future profitability of business, we can expect

    (A) the industry supply curve to shift to the right and prices to rise
    (B) the industry supply curve to shift to the right and prices to fall
    (C) the industry supply curve to shift to the left and prices to rise
    (D) the industry supply curve to shift to the left and prices to fall
    (E) the demand to rise and prices to rise

36. Which of the following would raise the current equilibrium price of a good?

    (A) an expectation on the part of consumers that future prices will be lower than present prices
    (B) an expectation on the part of consumers that future prices will be higher than present prices
    (C) fewer consumers and more producers
    (D) an increase in the price of a complementary good
    (E) a decrease in the price of a substitute good

37. Which of the following best describes the characteristics of a pure public good?

    (A) a good that is nonexclusive and nonrival
    (B) a good that is neither nonexclusive nor nonrival
    (C) a good that is nonexclusive but is rival
    (D) a good that is nonrival but is exclusive
    (E) a good that has both positive and negative externalities

38. If an increase in the price of one good decreases the demand for another good, then these two goods are

    (A) normal goods
    (B) inferior goods
    (C) public goods
    (D) complementary goods
    (E) substitute goods

39. Which of the following is most likely to increase the demand for widget makers?

    (A) an increase in the wages of widget makers
    (B) a decrease in the wages of widget makers
    (C) an increase in the supply of widget makers
    (D) an increase in the price of widgets
    (E) a decrease in the price of widgets

40. If a perfectly competitive market experiences an increase in demand what will happen to price, quantity produced, and profits of a single firm in that market in the short run?

	Price	Quantity	Profit
(A)	decrease	decrease	decrease
(B)	decrease	increase	increase
(C)	no change	decrease	increase
(D)	no change	increase	increase
(E)	increase	increase	increase

41. If the demand for a product is price inelastic and a government imposes an excise tax on that product, which of the following is most likely to result?

    (A) a relatively large decrease in use and a relatively large increase in government revenue
    (B) a relatively large decrease in use and a relatively small increase in government revenue
    (C) a relatively small decrease in use and a relatively large increase in government revenue
    (D) a relatively small decrease in use and a relatively small increase in government revenue
    (E) a relatively large increase in use and a relatively large decrease in government revenue

42. In the resource (or factor) market, what would be the most likely result of an increase in worker productivity and at the same time an increase in the price of the product?

    (A)   an increase in the demand for labor
    (B)   a decrease in the demand for labor
    (C)   an increase in the demand for labor and the supply of labor
    (D)   a decrease in the supply of labor
    (E)   an indeterminate effect on the demand for labor

Question 43 refers to the figure below.

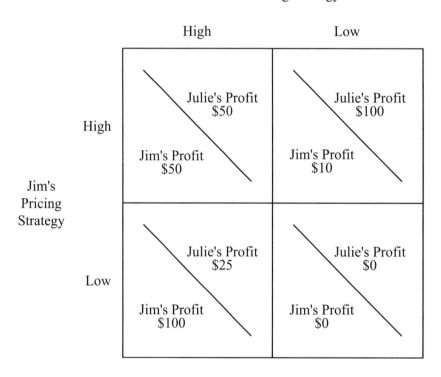

43. Based on the information in the figure above,

    (A)   Jim has a dominant strategy and Julie does not
    (B)   Julie has a dominant strategy and Jim does not
    (C)   neither Jim nor Julie have a dominant strategy
    (D)   both Jim and Julie have a dominant strategy
    (E)   no conclusion can be accurately made about strategic decision making based on the information in the figure above

44. When police apprehend suspects in a crime they typically separate them and offer incentives to confess. In economics the study of the ensuing strategies and outcomes is called

    (A) game theory
    (B) the paradox of value
    (C) diminishing marginal utility
    (D) diminishing marginal returns
    (E) negative externalities

Questions 45 – 46 refer to the figure below.

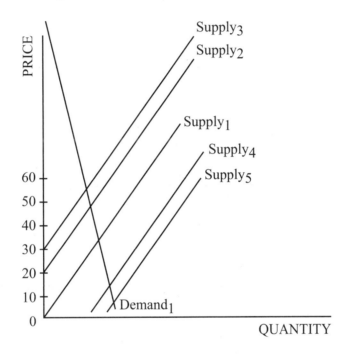

45. Refer to the graph above. Which shift correctly demonstrates the effect of the government imposing a $20 tax on the production of this good?

    (A) Supply$_1$ to Supply$_2$
    (B) Supply$_2$ to Supply$_1$
    (C) Supply$_1$ to Supply$_3$
    (D) Supply$_1$ to Supply$_4$
    (E) Supply$_1$ to Supply$_5$

46. Based on the information in the graph above, which of the following is correct?

    (A) consumers would pay most of the tax
    (B) producers would pay most of the tax
    (C) consumers and producers would share equally in paying the tax
    (D) the equilibrium price would increase by more than the tax
    (E) the government would pay the tax

47. If two competing firms are jointly concerned about the pricing strategy of the other firm in determining their own profit maximizing price and output decision, they are mostly likely competing in which of the following markets?

    (A) perfect competition
    (B) monopolistic competition
    (C) oligopoly
    (D) single-price monopoly
    (E) price-discriminating monopoly

Question 48 refers to the table below.

Labor

	0	1	2	3
1		100	200	500
2		200	300	600
3		300	400	700

Capital

Figures in the table represent output.

48. The firm in the table above has a production process characterized by

    (A) decreasing returns to labor, and increasing returns to capital
    (B) constant returns to labor, and constant returns to capital
    (C) increasing returns to labor, and constant returns to capital
    (D) increasing returns to capital, and increasing returns to labor
    (E) constant returns to scale, and constant returns to labor

49. A single-price monopolist has a price

    (A) equal to its marginal revenue
    (B) greater than its marginal revenue
    (C) less than its marginal revenue
    (D) equal to marginal cost
    (E) less than marginal cost

Question 50 refers to the figure below.

50. The Long-Run Average Cost curve above demonstrates

   (A) economies of scale
   (B) diseconomies of scale
   (C) constant returns to scale
   (D) opportunity cost
   (E) diminishing returns

_____

51. The Econville grocery store recently put up-chuck steak on sale. The result of the sale was that the store experienced a significant increase in their revenue from the sale of up-chuck steak even though they were selling it for a lower price. From this information we can conclude that

   (A) up-chuck steak is an inferior good
   (B) up-chuck steak is a normal good
   (C) the demand for up-chuck steak is price elastic
   (D) the demand for up-chuck steak is price inelastic
   (E) the demand for up-chuck steak is income elastic

52. The graph that portrays the relationship between the cumulative percentage of income on one axis and the cumulative percentage of families on the other axis is called the

   (A) Lorenz curve
   (B) Laffer curve
   (C) production possibilities curve
   (D) marginal revenue product curve
   (E) efficiency loss curve

Question 13 refers to the graph below.

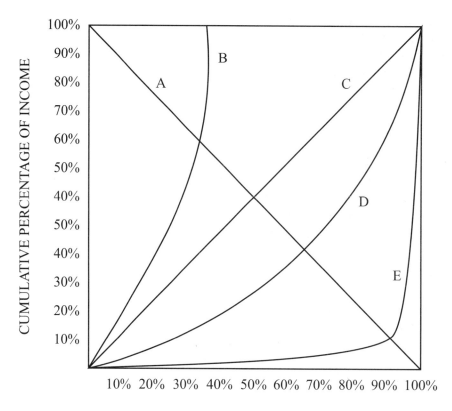

CUMULATIVE PERCENTAGE OF INCOME

CUMULATIVE PERCENTAGE OF POPULATION

53. Using the information in the graph above, the most equitable distribution of income is demonstrated on curve

   (A) A
   (B) B
   (C) C
   (D) D
   (E) E

---

54. A firm wishing to use the least-cost combination of labor and capital to produce a given output would employ more labor if

   (A) marginal product of labor/price of labor > marginal product of capital/price of capital
   (B) marginal product of labor/price of labor < marginal product of capital/price of capital
   (C) marginal revenue product of labor/price of labor < marginal revenue product of capital/ price of capital
   (D) marginal revenue product of labor/price of labor = marginal revenue product of capital/price of capital
   (E) marginal product of labor/price of labor = marginal product of capital/price of capital

55. Which of the following would increase the supply of a good?

    (A) an increase in the price of the good
    (B) an increase in the demand for the good
    (C) an increase in the price of a substitute good
    (D) a decrease in the price of a complementary good
    (E) a decrease in the cost of producing the good

56. If producing a good creates costs that accrue to neither the consumer nor the producer of the good

    (A) the market is still efficient and will continue to correctly allocate resources
    (B) the market is inefficient and will over allocate resources to the production of that good
    (C) the market is inefficient and will under allocate resources to the production of that good
    (D) the market is still efficient, but will over allocate resources to the production of that good
    (E) the market is still efficient, but will under allocate resources to the production of that good

57. Which of the following would increase the demand for a good?

    (A) a decrease in the price of the good
    (B) an increase in the price of a substitute good
    (C) an increase in the price of a complementary good
    (D) an increase in the price of an independent good
    (E) an increase in the supply of the good

58. If you find that every time you hire an additional worker in your factory, while holding capital constant, output increases by 10 units of production, then you would correctly conclude that you are expressing

    (A) increasing marginal returns to labor
    (B) constant marginal returns to labor
    (C) diminishing marginal returns to labor
    (D) increasing marginal returns to scale
    (E) constant marginal returns to scale

59. Studies in Econville show that every time consumers experience an increase in their incomes, they buy less turkey. From this information, we can conclude that turkey is a(n)

    (A) superior good
    (B) normal good
    (C) inferior good
    (D) complementary good
    (E) substitute good

60. In the resource (or factor) market, what would be the most certain result of an increase in worker productivity and an increase in the price of the product at the same time?

   (A) marginal revenue product of labor would increase
   (B) marginal revenue product of labor would decrease
   (C) marginal revenue product of labor would be indeterminate
   (D) marginal revenue product of labor would increase and the marginal resource cost of labor would increase
   (E) marginal revenue product of labor would increase but the marginal resource cost of labor would decrease

Free-Response Questions

1. Jimmy Charles Inc. is a monopolistic competitor operating in long-run equilibrium.

   (a) Draw a correctly labeled graph to demonstrate this long-run equilibrium position:
   (b) On the graph you drew in part (a), identify each of the following:
   - (i)   the point of allocative efficiency
   - (ii) the point of productive (technical) efficiency
   - (iii) the break-even point
   - (iv) the maximum profit point
   (c) Explain what will happen to each of the following in the short run, if there is an increase in market demand for the product being produced by Jimmy Charles Inc.
   - (i) profits of a typical firm in this industry
   - (ii) profits of a typical firm in this industry in the long run

2. Peanut butter and cashew butter are substitute goods. There is a drought that significantly decreases only the harvest of peanuts. For each of the following draw correctly labeled supply and demand curves to demonstrate the effect of the peanut blight on:

   (a) the peanut market
   (b) the cashew market
   (c) the market for peanut harvesting machinery
   (d) the market for cashew workers

3. The Elizabeth Company is the sole producer of fine replacement China. Answer each of the following for the Elizabeth Company:

   (a) In what market structure does the Elizabeth Company operate? Explain.
   (b) How will the Elizabeth Company determine its profit-maximizing level of output and the price it charges?
   (c) If the Elizabeth Company experiences an increase in the amount it pays for liability insurance, which does not depend on the quantity sold, explain how that will affect each of the following:
   - (i)   the price it charges for its product
   - (ii) the quantity it will offer for sale
   - (iii) the profits experienced

Macroeconomics: Unit I

Basic Concepts & Macroeconomic Indicators

1. The "central economic problem" faced by all economies is the result of

   (A) unequal income distribution
   (B) scarcity
   (C) globalization
   (D) technological change
   (E) global warming

2. Which of the following would be considered a macroeconomic issue as opposed to a microeconomic issue?

   (A) resource allocation
   (B) the determination of a product's price
   (C) the determination of the profit maximizing equilibrium for a monopoly
   (D) the determination of the full employment level of GDP
   (E) correction for positive or negative externalities

3. Which of the following is not a widely recognized goal of United States economic policy?

   (A) economic growth
   (B) price stability
   (C) full employment
   (D) maximum production
   (E) all of the above are recognized as economic goals of the United States

4. Which of the following sets identifies a leakage from the circular flow and an injection into the circular flow, respectively?

   (A) savings, taxes
   (B) taxes, savings
   (C) savings, investment
   (D) investment, savings
   (E) investment, exports

5. The types of unemployment include all of the following EXCEPT

   (A) frictional
   (B) cyclical
   (C) seasonal
   (D) nominal
   (E) structural

96

6. An increase in the Consumer Price Index from 200 to 225 would indicate an annual rate of measured inflation of

   (A) 1.3%
   (B) 12.5%
   (C) 25%
   (D) 200%
   (E) 225%

7. If actual inflation is more than expected inflation, which of the following groups will most certainly benefit?

   (A) lenders
   (B) borrowers
   (C) minorities
   (D) women
   (E) men

8. Which of the following is recognized as a valid criticism of the current practice of measuring unemployment?

   (A) Discouraged workers are counted in the total and therefore the published number overstates the actual amount of unemployment.
   (B) Discouraged workers are not counted in the total and therefore the published number understates the actual amount of unemployment.
   (C) Inflation is not factored in, thereby making the published numbers nominal and not real values.
   (D) Inflation is figured in, therefore the published numbers are real and not nominal.
   (E) All published numbers are susceptible to variations by season.

9. Gross Domestic Product measurements include

   (A) the purchase of a ticket to attend a rock concert from a scalper
   (B) the purchase of a rare antique coin
   (C) the purchase of a 1957 Chevy "classic car"
   (D) the purchase of a new car
   (E) a contribution to your IRA account

10. If Marie's annual income rose from $20,000 to $40,000 per year while the consumer price index rose from 200 to 300, we could conclude that she experienced which of the following combination of events?

	Nominal Income	Real Income
(A)	increase	increase
(B)	increase	constant
(C)	increase	decrease
(D)	constant	constant
(E)	decrease	decrease

Questions 11 – 14 refer to the graph below.

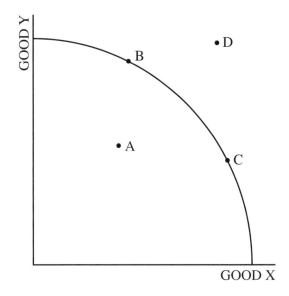

11. Based on the graph above, a point like A would demonstrate

    (A)   inflation
    (B)   stagflation
    (C)   unemployment
    (D)   an unattainable level of production
    (E)   the effect of globalization

12. Based on the graph above, a point like D would demonstrate

    (A)   inflation
    (B)   stagflation
    (C)   unemployment
    (D)   an unattainable level of production
    (E)   the effect of globalization

13. Based on the graph above, a movement from B to C would demonstrate which of the following economic principles?

    (A)   equilibrium
    (B)   opportunity cost
    (C)   profit maximization
    (D)   inflation
    (E)   unemployment

14. Based on the graph above, movement from C to A could be the result of

    (A) increased unemployment
    (B) increased efficiency
    (C) increased technology
    (D) increased discovery of resources
    (E) increased international trade

    _____

15. If measured inflation is less than actual inflation in a country that has indexed wages to the inflation measure then

    (A) workers will benefit
    (B) workers will be hurt
    (C) there is inflationary pressure built into the economy
    (D) the economy will eliminate future inflation
    (E) employers will be hurt

16. The concept of a "full-employment unemployment rate" or a "natural rate of unemployment" would be embodied in which of the following statements?

    (A) frictional unemployment is zero
    (B) structural unemployment is zero
    (C) seasonal unemployment is zero
    (D) cyclical unemployment is zero
    (E) all four of the above types of unemployment are zero

17. The following list of films are ranked by box office receipts. Their dates of release and the GDP deflator for these years are also listed. The top three for each of the following categories, respectively, would be

    1. Mrs. Peabody's Beach $100 million   1935   .10 GDP deflator
    2. San Antonio Redemption $300 million   1947   .50 GDP deflator
    3. Christine $400 million   1998   1.00 GDP deflator

	Nominal	Real
(A)	1, 2, 3	3, 2, 1
(B)	3, 2, 1	1, 2, 3
(C)	3, 2, 1	2, 1, 3
(D)	3, 2, 1	3, 1, 2
(E)	3, 2, 1	2, 3, 1

18. Turn of the 21st century benchmarks for unemployment, the inflation rate, and real GDP growth are

    (A) 0, 0, 0
    (B) 2%, 3%, 4%
    (C) 4-5%, 2-3%, 3-3.5%
    (D) 6-7%, 3-4%, 3.5-4%
    (E) 7-8%, 4-5%, 4-5%

19. The components of GDP from an expenditures perspective include

    (A) Consumption + Investment + Government Spending + Net Exports
    (B) Consumption + Investment + Net Exports + Depreciation
    (C) Savings + Taxes + Imports + Exports
    (D) Imports + Velocity + Exports + Income
    (E) Government Spending + Taxes + Reserve Requirement + Discount Rate

20. Which of the following are true about the effect of unanticipated inflation?

    (A) It reallocates income from one group to another.
    (B) It helps people who are in debt.
    (C) It hurts people who are on fixed incomes.
    (D) It hurts people who have loaned money to others.
    (E) All of the above are correct statements about the effects of unanticipated inflation.

21. With an annual rate of inflation of 7%, it would take how many years for prices to double?

    (A) 7
    (B) 10
    (C) 12
    (D) 15
    (E) 20

22. The specific name for a period of time during which the rate of inflation slows to a lower level of inflation is

    (A) inflation
    (B) deflation
    (C) recession
    (D) disinflation
    (E) hyperinflation

23. Which of the following are generally regarded as valid reasons for GDP over or under-stating social welfare?

    (A) non-market activities
    (B) the value of leisure time
    (C) product improvement
    (D) positive or negative externalities
    (E) all of the above

24. The combination of simultaneously high rates of unemployment and inflation is called

    (A) inflation
    (B) recession
    (C) depression
    (D) stagflation
    (E) slow growth

25. Which of the following most accurately represents the "economic bias" of United States economists toward free trade?

    (A) free trade is desirable as it extends our production possibility curve
    (B) free trade is desirable as it contracts our production possibility curve
    (C) free trade is undesirable as it extends our production possibility curve
    (D) free trade is undesirable as it increases inflation
    (E) free trade is undesirable as it restricts economic growth

26. Which of the following would not be a valid reason why GDP might *not* measure a nation's standard of living?

    (A) psychic income
    (B) the value of leisure time
    (C) unpaid household production
    (D) the fact that it only counts final production
    (E) income distribution

Free-Response Questions

1. Draw and correctly label a business cycle graph. On your graph identify each of the following:

   (a)   A peak, a trough, a contraction, and an expansion.
   (b)   The area, or point, where unemployment is most likely to be a problem.
   (c)   The area, or point, where inflation is most likely to be a problem.
   (d)   The area, or point, where the economy is most likely to experience "full employment."
   (e)   At the point (or area) you identified in part D, how would you define "full employment"?

2. The numbers in the table below identify how a typical economics student spends money.

| | Quantity Consumed | | |
Item	2008, 2009, 2010	2008 Price Each	2010 Price Each
Books	6	$125	$150
Food	10	$10	$12
Entertainment	2	$15	$20
Recreation	3	$100	$125

   Given this information complete each of the following:

   (a)   Construct a price index for this student for 2008 and 2010.
   (b)   Calculate the amount of inflation this student is experiencing.
   (c)   Calculate the annual rate of inflation.
   (d)   Compare the rate of inflation this student is experiencing to the rate that the United States typically experiences and make a comparison.

3. Identify two ways to calculate GDP.

   (a)   Why would GDP be the same when calculated either way?
   (b)   List two things that a typical consumer might buy that are not included in either method of calculation.
   (c)   List two reasons why GDP might not accurately measure a nation's standard of living.

102

Macroeconomics: Unit II

Business Cycles and Fiscal Policy

Question 1 refers to the graph below.

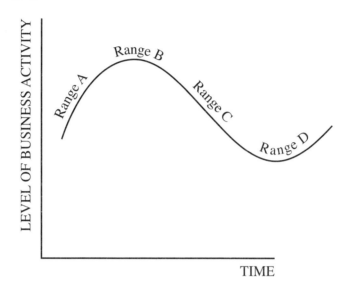

1. The correct labels for the four ranges in the graph above starting with Range A would be

   (A) peak, contraction, trough, expansion
   (B) contraction, trough, expansion, peak
   (C) trough, expansion, peak, contraction
   (D) expansion, peak, contraction, trough
   (E) trough, contraction, peak, expansion

   _____

2. Which of the following would be counted as consumption spending as opposed to investment spending?

   (A) new home construction
   (B) a net change in inventories
   (C) new machinery built
   (D) a new car purchase by a consumer
   (E) all of these would be consumption

103

3. An automobile that was produced in 2008 and sold in 2009 would be counted as _____ in 2008 and _____ in 2009.

   (A) consumption, consumption
   (B) investment, investment
   (C) consumption, investment
   (D) investment, consumption
   (E) consumption, government

4. Net domestic product is less than gross domestic product by an amount equal to

   (A) income taxes
   (B) indircct business taxes
   (C) depreciation
   (D) interest
   (E) inflation

5. Purposeful attempts by the federal government to act in a counter-cyclical manner are called

   (A) economics
   (B) fiscal policy
   (C) monetary policy
   (D) incomes policy
   (E) destabilization policy

6. Contractionary fiscal policy is most appropriate as a response to

   (A) recession
   (B) depression
   (C) stagflation
   (D) inflation
   (E) deflation

7. Which of the following would be a contractionary discretionary fiscal policy measure?

   (A) increasing the reserve requirement
   (B) making more payments to recipients of unemployment compensation
   (C) people paying higher taxes due to "bracket creep" associated with the progressive income tax
   (D) increasing the personal income tax rate
   (E) decreasing the personal income tax rate

Question 8 refers to the graph below.

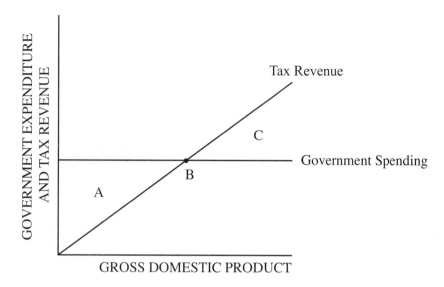

8. Based on the graph above, A, B, and C respectively represent a budget

   (A)   surplus, in balance, deficit
   (B)   in balance, deficit, surplus
   (C)   deficit, in balance, surplus
   (D)   deficit, surplus, in balance
   (E)   surplus, deficit, in balance

   _____

9. An advocate of a supply-side fiscal policy would argue for

   (A)   tax cuts to spur savings and investment
   (B)   tax increases to spur savings and investment
   (C)   government spending increases to spur savings and investment
   (D)   government spending decreases to increase interest rates
   (E)   budget deficiets to combat recession and budget surpluses to combat inflation

10. An advocate of a demand-side (Keynesian) fiscal policy would argue for

   (A)   tax cuts to spur savings and investment
   (B)   tax increases to spur savings and investment
   (C)   government spending increases to spur savings and investment
   (D)   government spending decreases to increase interest rates
   (E)   budget deficits to combat recession and budget surpluses to combat inflation

Question 11 refers to the graph below.

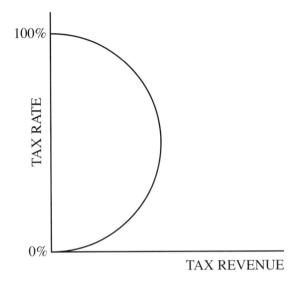

11. The Laffer curve above, purports to show that

(A) higher tax rates always lead to lower government revenue
(B) lower tax rates always lead to lower government revenue
(C) higher tax rates always lead to higher government revenue
(D) beyond some point higher tax rates lead to lower government revenue
(E) beyond some point higher tax rates lead to even higher tax rates

––––––––––––––––––

12. Proponents of an incomes policy would cite as one of their basic tenants

(A) inflation is perpetuated by expectations of inflation
(B) advocacy of wage-price controls
(C) a need to break the link between wage increases and price increases
(D) all of the above
(E) none of the above

13. If the marginal propensity to consume is .8 and the federal government increases spending by $100 billion and increases taxes by $100 billion to pay for it, which of the following correctly describes the result?

(A) $100 billion increase in GDP
(B) $100 billion decrease in GDP
(C) no change in GDP
(D) $500 billion increase in GDP
(E) $500 billion decrease in GDP

14. The national debt and a budget deficit respectively are referred to by economists as

    (A) a stock, and a flow
    (B) a flow, and a stock
    (C) both are flows
    (D) both are stocks
    (E) neither is a flow or a stock

15. The level of business activity over time is portrayed on a graph called

    (A) the Laffer curve
    (B) the Phillips curve
    (C) the business cycle
    (D) the cyclical trend
    (E) the secular trend

16. Over time economies such as the United States have shown a long-term growth trend. This trend for real GDP to grow over time is referred to as

    (A) the Laffer curve
    (B) the Phillips curve
    (C) the business cycle
    (D) the cyclical trend
    (E) the secular trend

17. A Classical economist would argue for

    (A) the active use of discretionary fiscal policy to correct for short-term business cycle fluctuations
    (B) the active use of discretionary monetary policy to correct for short-term business cycle fluctuations
    (C) the active use of both fiscal and monetary policy to correct for short-term business cycle fluctuations
    (D) leaving short-term business cycle fluctuations to take care of themselves and would discourage the use of discretionary policies to correct these short-term fluctuations
    (E) using discretionary fiscal and monetary policies to correct for short-term business cycle fluctuations only to combat inflation and not to combat recession.

18. A decrease in which of the following is likely to have the largest and the most immediate expansionary effect on an economy?

    (A) taxes
    (B) transfer payments
    (C) government spending
    (D) entitlement programs
    (E) federal government budget deficit

19. A decrease in which of the following would increase the numerical value of the simple spending multiplier?

    (A) marginal propensity to consume
    (B) marginal propensity to save
    (C) budget deficit
    (D) budget surplus
    (E) national debt

20. Which of the following combinations would have the greatest expansionary effect on an economy?

	Taxes	Government Spending	Transfer Payments
(A)	increase	increase	increase
(B)	increase	increase	decrease
(C)	increase	decrease	decrease
(D)	decrease	decrease	decrease
(E)	decrease	increase	increase

21. The simple spending multiplier is correctly expressed as

    (A) 1/MPS
    (B) 1/MPC
    (C) 1/MPS + MPC
    (D) MPS/MPC
    (E) MPC/MPS

22. Given an MPC of .80, the maximum amount by which GDP could increase with an increase in government spending of $100 is

    (A) $20
    (B) $80
    (C) $100
    (D) $125
    (E) $500

Free-Response Questions

1. Analyze the economy described by the following figures:

   Unemployment rate   8%
   Inflation rate   3%
   Annual rate of GDP growth   2%

   (a) What is the biggest problem this economy is facing?
   (b) What would be the appropriate fiscal policy to combat this problem?

2. Answer each of the following for an economy with a marginal propensity to consume of 80% and which is operating at a level of GDP that is $1000 less than the desired level.

   (a) Identify two specific fiscal policy tools that could be used to increase GDP to the desired level.
   (b) Identify the appropriate size of each of the fiscal policy measures you listed in part A.

3. The government of Econville has decided to build a bridge connecting the Saltwater side of Econville to Freshwater side of Econville and this project is expected to cost $100 billion. The government does NOT want to run a deficit to complete the project. Complete each of the following in regards to the proposed bridge project:

   (a) If the government of Econville is committed to the bridge project, how could they complete it without having a budget deficit in the short run?
   (b) What would be the effect on the economy of Econville of the bridge project? Why?

Macroeconomics: Unit III

Money, Banking, and Monetary Policy

1. A type of money that has an intrinsic value in and of itself, like gold, is referred to as

   (A) bank notes
   (B) reserve notes
   (C) fiat money
   (D) commodity money
   (E) Gresham's money

2. The effect of contractionary monetary policy on interest rates and GDP respectively is

   (A) increase, increase
   (B) increase, decrease
   (C) decrease, decrease
   (D) decrease, constant
   (E) decrease, increase

3. The "quantity theory of money" is best expressed by which of the following?

   (A) marginal propensity to consume = marginal propensity to save
   (B) gross domestic product = consumption + investment + government spending + net exports
   (C) 1 / reserve requirement
   (D) money supply X velocity of money = price level X output
   (E) interest = principal X rate X time

Question 4 refers to the graph below.

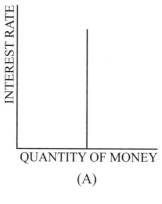

(A)

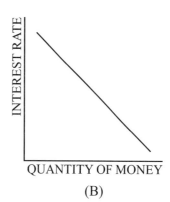

(B)

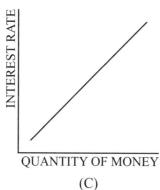

(C)

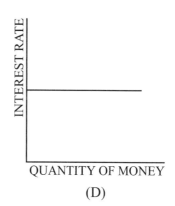

(D)

4. In the graphs above, the asset demand and the transactions demand for money would be shown, respectively, as

   (A)　A, B
   (B)　A, C
   (C)　A, D
   (D)　B, A
   (E)　B, D

5. A fractional reserve system with a reserve requirement of 10% into which a new deposit of $1,000 is made, could experience a maximum change in the money supply of

   (A)　an increase of $1,000
   (B)　an increase of $9,000
   (C)　an increase of $10,000
   (D)　a decrease of $10,000
   (E)　a decrease of $9,000

6. Which of the following combinations represent the monetary policy that would decrease real GDP the most?

	Open Market Operations	Reserve Requirement
(A)	sell	decrease
(B)	buy	decrease
(C)	sell	increase
(D)	buy	increase
(E)	sell	keep constant

Question 7 refers to the graphs below.

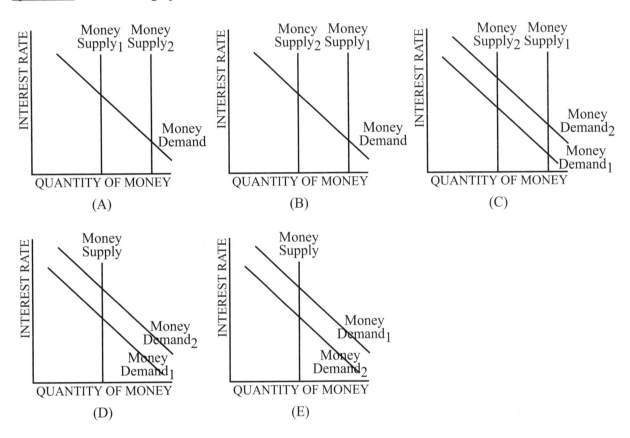

7. Which of the graphs above demonstrate the appropriate monetary policy to achieve increased consumer spending on durable goods?

(A) A
(B) B
(C) C
(D) D
(E) E

8. Money definitions would include all of the following components EXCEPT

   (A) means of exchange
   (B) store of value
   (C) unit of account
   (D) based on gold standard
   (E) a reason to barter

9. Gresham's Law states that

   (A) good money drives bad money out of circulation
   (B) bad money drives good money out of circulation
   (C) more dollars chase fewer goods
   (D) more goods chase fewer dollars
   (E) $MV = PY$

10. The money supply in the United States is controlled by

   (A) Congress
   (B) the President
   (C) the federal government
   (D) the Federal Reserve System
   (E) the market

11. Which of the following would be included in the M1 definition of the money supply?

   I. $100 in the vault of, and owned by, the Chicago Federal Reserve Bank
   II. $100 in the vault of, and owned by, the Bank of Homewood
   III. $100 in your wallet
   IV. $100 in your checking account at the Homewood-Flossmoor Federal Credit Union

   (A) I only
   (B) I and II only
   (C) III and IV only
   (D) II, III, and IV only
   (E) I, II, III, and IV

12. If you signed a 60-month fixed-rate loan contract with an interest rate of 8% in an economy with an inflationary expectation of 3%, we could accurately conclude

	The Real Interest Rate is	The Nominal Interest Rate is
(A)	3%	5%
(B)	5%	8%
(C)	8%	5%
(D)	8%	11%
(E)	11%	8%

13. The relationship that exists between the purchasing power of the dollar and the Consumer Price Index is

    (A) direct
    (B) inverse
    (C) as likely to be either direct or inverse
    (D) no relationship exists at all
    (E) one to one

Question 14 refers to the graph below.

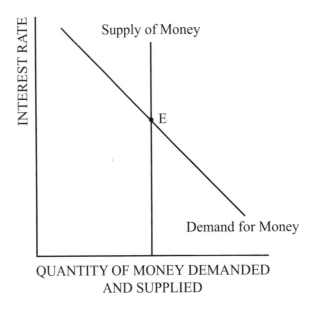

14. Beginning at equilibrium E in the graph above, if there is a sudden decrease in the Supply of Money, which of the following is the chain of events that will result?

    (A) a temporary shortage of money followed by an increase in interest rates
    (B) a temporary shortage of money followed by a decrease in interest rates
    (C) a temporary surplus of money followed by an increase in interest rates
    (D) a temporary surplus of money followed by a decrease in interest rates
    (E) a permanent shortage of money with no adjustment in interest rates

15. The relationship between the amount of inflation a nation experiences and the level of independence of the central bank from the 1980's to the present is

    (A) direct
    (B) inverse
    (C) as likely to be direct as inverse
    (D) neither
    (E) no nation has an independent central bank

16. When the Fed engages in the expansionary use of open market operations they are

    (A) selling government bonds
    (B) buying government bonds
    (C) increasing the reserve requirement
    (D) decreasing the reserve requirement
    (E) decreasing taxes

17. The most frequently used tool of monetary policy is

    (A) changes in the reserve requirement
    (B) changes in the discount rate
    (C) open market operations
    (D) changes in taxes
    (E) changes in government spending

18. Which of the following correctly depicts the Keynesian monetary policy transmission mechanism after an increase in the money supply?

    (A) a decrease in interest rates, followed by an increase in investment demand, followed by an increase in aggregate demand, followed by an increase in GDP
    (B) an increase in interest rates, followed by an increase in investment demand, followed by an increase in aggregate demand, followed by an increase in GDP
    (C) an increase in interest rates, followed by a decrease in investment demand, followed by an increase in aggregate demand, followed by an increase in GDP
    (D) an increase in interest rates, followed by a decrease in investment demand, followed by a decrease in aggregate demand, followed by an increase in GDP
    (E) an increase in interest rates, followed by a decrease in investment demand, followed by a decrease in aggregate demand, followed by a decrease in GDP

19. Which of the following correctly describes the relationship between real and nominal interest rates?

    (A) real + expected inflation = nominal
    (B) real – expected inflation = nominal
    (C) nominal + expected inflation = real
    (D) nominal and real are always equal
    (E) nominal + real = expected inflation

20. The simple money multiplier is correctly expressed as

    (A) 1/MPC
    (B) 1/MPS
    (C) 1/reserve requirement
    (D) 1/tax rate
    (E) reserve requirement X tax rate

21. The effect on interest rates of contractionary fiscal and monetary policies, respectively, are

    (A) increase, increase
    (B) increase, constant
    (C) increase, decrease
    (D) decrease, increase
    (E) decrease, decrease

22. Which of the following combinations would be the most contractionary?

	Reserve Requirement	Open Market Operations	Fed Funds Rate
(A)	increase	sell	increase
(B)	increase	buy	increase
(C)	decrease	sell	decrease
(D)	decrease	buy	decrease
(E)	decrease	sell	increase

Question 23 refers to the graphs below.

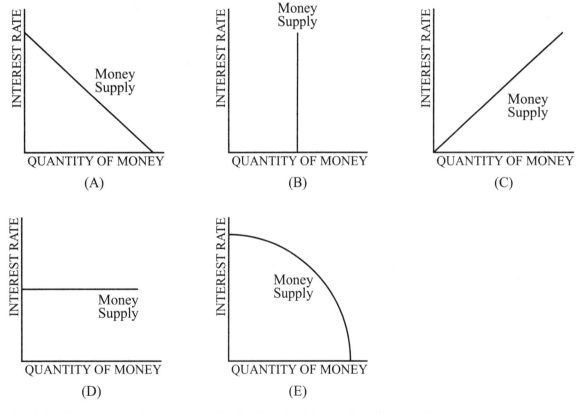

23. Which of the graphs above accurately displays the Money Supply curve?

    (A) A
    (B) B
    (C) C
    (D) D
    (E) E

24. The factor that would most likely render the discretionary use of monetary policy as a tool of stabilization policy unacceptable

    (A) the inability of the Federal Reserve to quickly act
    (B) the inability of the Federal Reserve to reach consensus
    (C) the inability of the Federal Reserve and Congress to agree on the appropriate policy to implement
    (D) the uncertainty as to the time lags involved between the implementation of policy and the resulting effect on the economy
    (E) the uncertainty as to which tool of policy to actually use

25. Expansionary monetary policy would be most effective to combat

    (A) recession
    (B) inflation
    (C) stagflation
    (D) expansion
    (E) peak

Free-Response Questions

1. Analyze the economy described by the following figures:

Unemployment rate	5%
Inflation rate	5%
Annual rate of GDP growth	7%

   (a)   What is the biggest problem facing this economy?
   (b)   Identify two fiscal policy tools that could be used to combat this problem.
   (c)   Identify two monetary policy tools that could be used to combat this problem.

2. Assume the reserve requirement for a banking system is 20%. Under the typical assumptions corresponding with the money multiplier, if an autonomous injection of $10,000 is made, how will it affect:

   (a)   The initial required reserves of the individual bank into which this deposit is made?
   (b)   The initial excess reserves of the individual bank into which this deposit is made?
   (c)   Total deposits in the entire banking system after all of the repercussions of this injection?
   (d)   Are there any factors that might not allow this to work in the real world in the way economic theory might suggest? If so, what are they?

3. Draw and correctly label a graph of the money market. On your graph demonstrate each of the following:

   (a)   Identify the equilibrium interest rate.
   (b)   Explain if the rate you identified in part (a) is a nominal or real rate.
   (c)   On your graph demonstrate the effect of federal government engaging in a budget deficit reduction plan.
   (d)   On your graph demonstrate the effect of the Federal Reserve engaging in a contractionary monetary policy.

118

Macroeconomics: Unit IV

Aggregate Supply / Aggregate Demand

Questions 1 – 2 refer to the graph below.

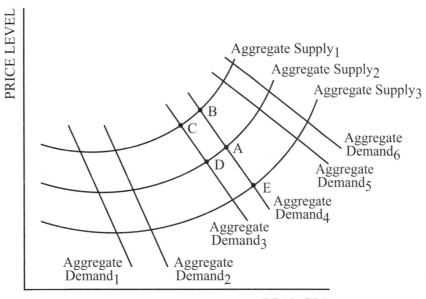

1. In the graph above, an optimistic view toward the future by consumers and an increase in expectations of profitability by business would result in a shift from

   (A) Aggregate Demand$_6$ to Aggregate Demand$_5$
   (B) Aggregate Demand$_3$ to Aggregate Demand$_4$
   (C) Aggregate Demand$_3$ to Aggregate Demand$_2$
   (D) Aggregate Supply$_1$ to Aggregate Supply$_2$
   (E) Aggregate Supply$_3$ to Aggregate Supply$_2$

2. In the graph above, beginning at equilibrium point A, stagflation could be demonstrated by a single curve shift that would result in a new equilibrium at point

   (A) A
   (B) B
   (C) C
   (D) D
   (E) E

119

3. A simultaneous and equally sized tax increase and spending increase by the federal government would have which of the following effects?

    (A)   increase the price level and increase real output
    (B)   increase the price level and decrease real output
    (C)   decrease in the price level and decrease in real output
    (D)   decrease in the price level and increase in real output
    (E)   no effect on price level or real output

4. An inward shift (to the left) in a production possibility curve would be most closely synonymous with a (n)

    (A)   incrcase in long-run aggregate supply
    (B)   decrease in long-run aggregate supply
    (C)   increase in aggregate demand
    (D)   decrease in aggregate demand
    (E)   decrease in capacity utilization rate

5. In the country of Laurenstan, an island nation previously closed to contact with the rest of the world, the citizens tend to spend 90% of any increase in income. Based on this, if a traveler from the outside were to visit and spend $5,000 on a newly produced product, the GDP of Laurenstan could increase by a maximum of

    (A) $5,000
    (B) $9,000
    (C) $10,000
    (D) $45,000
    (E) $50,000

6. Which of the following will increase aggregate demand?

    (A)   an increase in consumer indebtedness
    (B)   a decrease in excess capacity (unused capital)
    (C)   an increase in the price level
    (D)   an increase in taxes
    (E)   an increase in foreign national income

7. Which of the following will increase short-run aggregate supply?

    (A)   a decrease in consumer optimism
    (B)   a decrease in business optimism
    (C)   a decrease in the price level
    (D)   a decrease in business taxes
    (E)   a decrease in government spending

8. A series of natural disasters like fires, floods and earthquakes in the short run could cause

    (A)   demand shocks and inflation
    (B)   supply shocks and inflation
    (C)   demand shocks and deflation
    (D)   supply shocks and deflation
    (E)   non of the above to happen

Question 9 refers to the graph below.

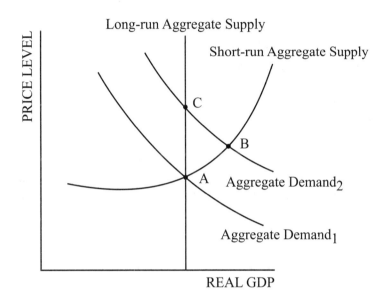

9. In the graph above, if the economy is presently operating at point B, in the absence of intervention, we can conclude that

    (A)   point B is the short-run equilibrium and long-run equilibrium will be established at point B
    (B)   point B is the short-run equilibrium and long-run equilibrium will be established at point A
    (C)   point B is the short-run equilibrium and long-run equilibrium will be established at point C
    (D)   point C is the short-run equilibrium and long-run equilibrium will be established at point C
    (E)   point A is the short-run equilibrium and long-run equilibrium will be established at point B

10. Which of the following explains the downward slope of an aggregate demand curve?

    (A)   increasing price level effect
    (B)   foreign purchases effect
    (C)   interest rate effect
    (D)   diminishing marginal utility effect
    (E)   production possibility effect

11. Cost-push and demand-pull inflation respectively would be caused by

    (A) increases in aggregate demand and increases in aggregate supply
    (B) increases in aggregate demand and decreases in aggregate supply
    (C) increases in aggregate supply and decreases in aggregate demand
    (D) decreases in aggregate supply and increases in aggregate demand
    (E) decreases in aggregate demand and decreases in aggregate supply

12. Based on findings of the Council of Economics Advisors to the President, the complex multiplier is

    (A) greater than the simple spending multiplier
    (B) less than the simple spending multiplier
    (C) equal to the simple spending multiplier
    (D) equal to the reserve requirement
    (E) equal to the simple money multiplier

13. A commonly cited shortcoming of the effectiveness of fiscal policy is that

    (A) the interest rate effect and the foreign purchases effect tend to support the policy action
    (B) the interest rate effect and the foreign purchases effect tend to run counter to the policy
    (C) the interest rate effect runs counter to the policy and the foreign purchases effect tends to support the policy
    (D) the interest rate effect supports the policy and the foreign purchases effect runs counter to the policy
    (E) the time lags that exist between implementation and effect are uncertain and varied

14. Limitations of expansionary fiscal policy would include all of the following EXCEPT

    (A) crowding out
    (B) net export effect
    (C) demand-pull inflation
    (D) offsetting savings (Ricardian equivalence)
    (E) uncertain time lags of the effect

15. If you believe that there is a short-run tradeoff between inflation and unemployment, which of the following economic concepts would be the basis of your belief?

    (A) Okun's law
    (B) Phillips curve
    (C) Gresham's law
    (D) Monetary rule
    (E) Keynesian economics

16. The concept of crowding out (or crowding in) is generally regarded as a limitation of the effectiveness of

    (A) fiscal policy
    (B) monetary policy
    (C) incomes policy
    (D) open-market operations
    (E) the balanced-budget multiplier

Question 17 refers to the graph below.

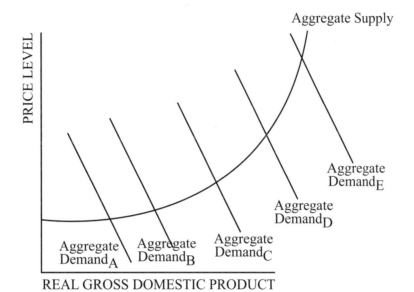

17. The intersection of which of the Aggregate Demand curves with the Aggregate Supply curve in the graph above best demonstrates an economy near full employment?

    (A) A
    (B) B
    (C) C
    (D) D
    (E) E

Question 18 refers to the graphs below.

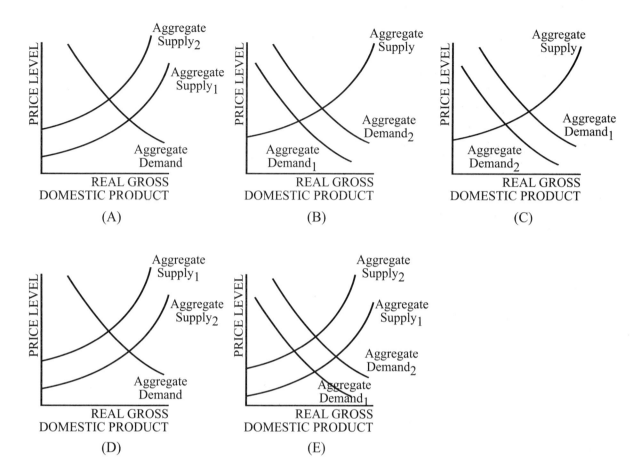

18. The effect of a simultaneous increase in government spending and the money supply would be correctly shown in which of the graphs above?

   (A) A
   (B) B
   (C) C
   (D) D
   (E) E

_____

19. The long-run aggregate supply curve is most similar to the

   (A) Phillips curve
   (B) Laffer curve
   (C) short-run aggregate supply curve
   (D) production possibility curve
   (E) investment demand curve

20. Which of the following most closely sums up the difference in views about macroeconomic stability of the Classical and Keynesian economists?

(A) the Classical view is that the economy is inherently unstable and needs active counter-cyclical policies to provide stability, while the Keynesian view is that the best course of action is to allow market forces through flexible wages and prices to correct for any short-run fluctuations

(B) the Keynesian view is that the economy is inherently unstable and needs active counter-cyclical policies to provide stability, while the Clasical view is that the best course of action is to allow market forces through flexible wages and prices to correct for any short-run fluctuations

(C) the Keynesian view favors the active use of fiscal policy to correct for short-run fluctuations in the economy, while the Classical view favors the active use of monetary policy to correct for short-run fluctuations in the economy

(D) both the Keynesian and Classical view is that the economy is inherently unstable and needs active counter-cyclical policies to provide stability

(E) both the Keynesian and Classical view is that the best course of action is to allow market forces through flexible wages and prices to correct for any short-run fluctuations

Question 21 refers to the graphs below.

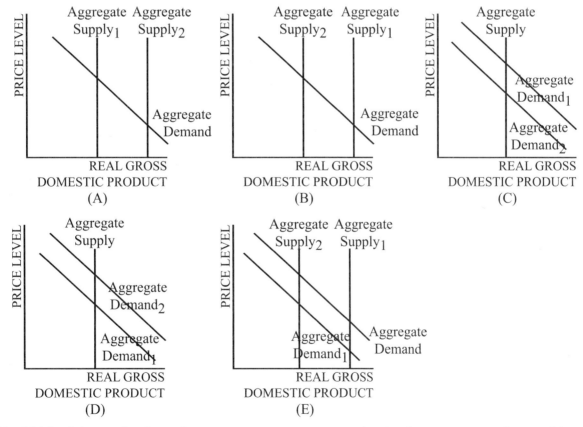

21. Which of the graphs above demonstrates an economy experiencing long-run economic growth?

(A) A
(B) B
(C) C
(D) D
(E) E

22. Which of the following represents valid potential limitations of the effectiveness of fiscal policy and monetary policy respectively?

    (A) crowding out, and a weak link between interest rate changes and investment changes
    (B) a weak link between interest rate changes and investment, and crowding out
    (C) the inability of congress to decide on the correct fiscal policy to use, and the inability of the Federal Reserve to decide on the correct monetary policy to use
    (D) crowding out, and crowding in
    (E) crowding in, and crowding out

23. If the federal government engages in a deficit reduction plan, what will be the effect of each of the following?

	Loanable Funds Market	Real Interest Rate
(A)	increase in demand	increase
(B)	decrease in demand	decrease
(C)	increase in supply	increase
(D)	decrease in supply	decrease
(E)	decrease in supply	increase

24. Which of the following is the most likely outcome of a simultaneous expansionary fiscal policy and an expansionary monetary policy?

	Interest Rate	Price Level	Real Output
(A)	increase	increase	increase
(B)	increase	decrease	decrease
(C)	decrease	decrease	decrease
(D)	indeterminate	decrease	decrease
(E)	indeterminate	increase	increase

Question 6 refers to the graph below.

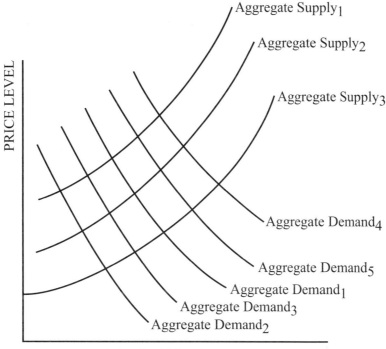

25. In the graph above, crowding in is shown by which of the following shifts?

    (A)   Aggregate Demand$_1$ to Aggregate Demand$_4$ to Aggregate Demand$_5$

    (B)   Aggregate Demand$_1$ to Aggregate Demand$_5$ to Aggregate Demand$_4$

    (C)   Aggregate Demand$_1$ to Aggregate Demand$_2$ to Aggregate Demand$_3$

    (D)   Aggregate Demand$_1$ to Aggregate Demand$_3$ to Aggregate Demand$_2$

    (E)   Aggregate Supply$_1$ to Aggregate Supply$_2$ toAggregate Supply$_3$

Free-Response Questions

1. Assume that the following figures represent the existing condition in an economy.

   Unemployment rate   4%
   Inflation rate   3%
   Annual rate of GDP growth   3.5%

   (a) Is this economy facing any economic problems as described by the data above? Explain.
   (b) Draw an aggregate supply and aggregate demand diagram to demonstrate the current condition for this economy.
   (c) On the diagram you drew for part B demonstrate the effect of the federal government engaging in a massive new nationwide road building project.
   (d) Analyze the effect of this massive new nationwide road building project on each of the following:
       (i) the level of output
       (ii) the level of unemployment
       (iii) the price level

2. Draw and correctly label a short-run Phillips curve. Demonstrate each of the following:

   (a) The effect of a rightward shift of the aggregate demand curve.
   (b) The effect of a leftward shift of the aggregate supply curve.

3. In an economy productivity has been increasing at a slower rate than nominal wages. Analyze the short run effects of this on:

   (a) Aggregate demand
   (b) Aggregate supply
   (c) Price level
   (d) Output
   (e) Employment

128

Macroeconomics: Unit V

International Economics

1. An exchange rate is best defined as

   (A) the rate at which goods are exchanged for money
   (B) the rate at which a nation's currency exchanges for gold
   (C) the price of one nation's currency from one year to the next
   (D) the price of one nation's currency expressed in terms of another nation's currency
   (E) the ratio between a nation's currency and its price level

Question 2 refers to the graphs below.

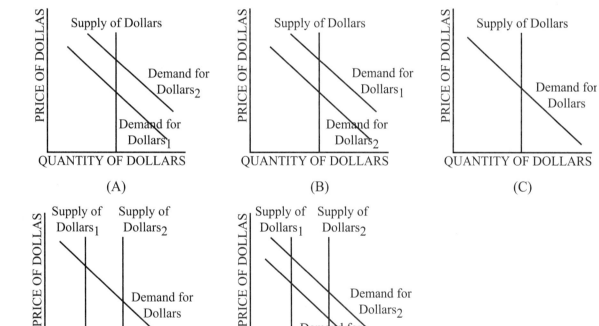

2. If interest rates in a country decreased, which of the graphs above shows the effect this would have on that nation's currency in the foreign exchange market?

   (A) A
   (B) B
   (C) C
   (D) D
   (E) E

129

3. An economist would point out that a nation that purposely pursues a policy of free trade does so

    (A) at a cost to society in general, but a possible benefit to some domestic producers
    (B) at a cost to some domestic producers, but a benefit to society in general
    (C) at a cost to society in general, and a cost to all domestic producers
    (D) with a benefit to all domestic producers and consumers
    (E) only if other nations reciprocate

4. Tariffs, quotas, and embargos are all forms of

    (A) incomes policy
    (B) fiscal policy
    (C) monetary policy
    (D) free trade
    (E) protectionism

5. If the nation of Econstan suddenly becomes a worldwide popular vacation destination for tourists, what could we expect to happen in the market for the Econstan unit of money, the moohlah?

    (A) the demand for the moohlah would increase
    (B) the demand for the moohlah would decrease
    (C) the supply of the moohlah would increase
    (D) the supply of the moohlah would decrease
    (E) the demand for and supply of the moohlah would not be affected

Questions 6 – 8 refer to the table below.

	Day 1	Day 2
U.S.	$2	$2
T.H.E.M.	£3	£4

6. Based on the information in the table above, we could conclude that from Day 1 to Day 2

    (A) the U.S. $ appreciated
    (B) the U.S. $ depreciated
    (C) the U.S. $ floated
    (D) the U.S. $ sunk
    (E) the U.S. $ was unaffected

7. Based on the information in the table above we could conclude that in Day 2, relative to Day 1

    (A) the U.S. will export more to T.H.E.M.
    (B) the U.S. will import more from T.H.E.M
    (C) the U.S. will import less from T.H.E.M.
    (D) T.H.E.M. will import more from the U.S.
    (E) T.H.E.M. will export less to the U.S.

8. Based on the information in the table above we could conclude that

  (A) the U.S. will certainly experience a recession
  (B) T.H.E.M. will certainly experience a recession
  (C) capital flows will enter the U.S. at a faster rate
  (D) capital flows will exit the U.S. at a faster rate
  (E) capital flows will not be affected

---

9. Which of the following combinations or circumstances would enable an economy to experience the most rapid rate of economic growth?

	Interest Rate	Savings	Capacity Utilization Rate
(A)	high	high	high
(B)	high	low	low
(C)	low	low	low
(D)	low	low	high
(E)	low	high	high

Question 10 refers to the graphs below.

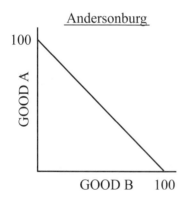
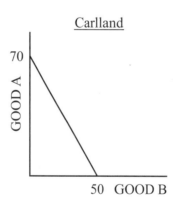

10. Based on the graphs above, which reflects the amounts that can be produced using all available resources, we can conclude that

  (A) Andersonburg has an absolute advantage in A only
  (B) Andersonburg has an absolute advantage in B only
  (C) Carlland has an absolute advantage in A only
  (D) Carlland has an absolute advantage in B only
  (E) Andersonburg has an absolute advantage in A and B

---

11. Economic growth would be best characterized by

 (A) a rightward shift in the production possibility curve and a rightward shift in the long-run aggregate supply curve
 (B) a leftward shift in the production possibility curve and a rightward shift in the long-run aggregate supply curve
 (C) a rightward shift in the production possibility curve and a leftward shift in the long-run aggregate supply curve
 (D) a leftward shift in the production possibility curve and a leftward shift in the long-run aggregate supply curve
 (E) an increase in nominal GDP over time

12. Which of the following would lead to increases in real GDP over time?

 (A) increases in taxes
 (B) increases in government spending
 (C) increases in the size of the labor force
 (D) increases in interest rates
 (E) decreases in government spending

13. The stance of most economists on international trade issues is

 (A) pro-free trade as it results in a more efficient allocation of resources
 (B) anti-free trade as it results in a less efficient allocation of resources
 (C) pro-protectionist as it results in a more efficient allocation of resources
 (D) as likely to be free trade as protectionist
 (E) noncommittal – few economists embrace one side or the other

14. Which of the following is not regarded as a trade barrier?

 (A) tariffs
 (B) quotas
 (C) embargos
 (D) General Agreement on Tariffs and Trade (GATT)
 (E) voluntary export restrictions

15. If the nation of Laurenstan found its central bank willing to finance increases in government spending by printing money, the most likely chain of events that would result is a(n)

 (A) depreciation of their currency, and a decrease in exports
 (B) depreciation of their currency, and an increase in exports
 (C) appreciation of their currency, and a decrease in exports
 (D) appreciation of their currency, and an increase in exports
 (E) appreciation of their currency, and no change in exports

16. A sudden increase in the worldwide popularity of Econ T-Shirts, an exclusive product of a Frankfort, Illinois based firm, would have what effect on the demand and supply for the dollar and its international value?

	Demand	Supply	International Value
(A)	no change	decrease	decrease
(B)	no change	decrease	increase
(C)	increase	no change	decrease
(D)	increase	no change	increase
(E)	decrease	increase	decrease

17. If the federal government suddenly engages in a dramatic expansionary fiscal policy move funded with the sale of government bonds, each of the following will be affected in what way?

	Loanable Funds Market	Value of Currency	Imports
(A)	demand decrease	decrease	decrease
(B)	demand increase	increase	increase
(C)	demand decrease	increase	increase
(D)	demand increase	increase	decrease
(E)	demand increase	decrease	increase

18. If a nation experiences an increase in real interest rates while those of other countries remain constant, we could expect

    (A) the value of that nation's currency to decrease
    (B) the value of that nation's currency to be unaffected
    (C) the long-run aggregate supply curve of that nation to decrease
    (D) the amount of that nation's imports to decrease
    (E) the amount of that nation's exports to decrease

19. Which of the following would contribute to a nation having a current account deficit?

    (A) an increase in imports
    (B) an increase in exports
    (C) an active fiscal policy
    (D) an active monetary policy
    (E) a domestic recession

20. If foreigners suddenly find touring the United States increasingly popular, which of the following will most likely occur?

    (A) an increase in the demand for the dollar and an increase in its price in foreign exchange markets
    (B) an increase in the demand for the dollar and a decrease in its price in foreign exchange markets
    (C) a decrease in the demand for the dollar and an increase in its price in foreign exchange markets
    (D) a decrease in the demand for the dollar and a decrease in its price in foreign exchange markets
    (E) no change in the demand for the dollar or in its price in foreign exchange markets

Free-Response Questions

1. List one fiscal policy and one monetary policy action that, if enacted, would correct a recessionary episode for an economy.

    (a) Explain how each would affect the price level and output.
    (b) Explain the effect the price level change would have on imports and exports.
    (c) Explain the effect the output level change would have on imports and exports.
    (d) Explain the effect of the fiscal policy move on the interest rate.
    (e) Explain the effect of the monetary policy move on the interest rate.

2. Based on the information in the table below answer each of the following:

Exchange Rates

	U.S. Dollar	Econville Peso
Year 1	1	4
Year 2	1	3

    (a) What has happened to the value of the Dollar from Year 1 to Year 2?
    (b) What effect will this change have on U.S. exports and imports to and from Econville?
    (c) What effect will this change have on the price of American made goods in the U.S.?
    (d) What effect will this change have on the U.S. balance of trade?

3. Draw and correctly label a diagram of aggregate supply and aggregate demand diagram.

    (a) On your diagram identify potential (full employment) output.
    (b) Explain how the government might use a tax policy to promote long-run economic growth.
    (c) Explain how a central bank might encourage long-run economic growth.
    (d) Draw a production possibility curve for consumer goods and capital goods to show how the policy measure in either B or C would affect the nation's production possibilities curve.

Macroeconomics

Sample Examination I

1. Which of the following would be counted in the calculation of real GDP?

   (A) a consumer purchasing 100 shares of stock
   (B) a consumer buying a previously owned computer
   (C) a parts company selling its product to an assembly company
   (D) a business increasing its inventory of finished goods
   (E) a domestic producer buying parts from a foreign supplier

Questions 2 – 3 refer to the graph below.

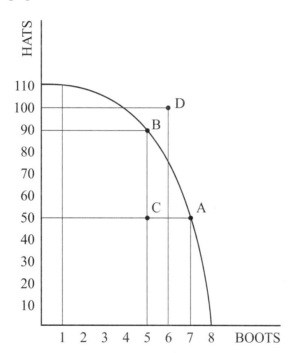

2. Which of the following could cause the movement from point A to point B in the production possibility curve shown above?

   (A) an increase in consumer preference for hats
   (B) an increase in consumer preference for boots
   (C) an increase in production costs
   (D) a decrease in production costs
   (E) an increase in the technology used to make hats and boots

135

3. Based on the graph above, which of the following is correct?

    (A)   the opportunity cost of moving from point A to point C is two boots
    (B)   the opportunity cost of moving from point A to point B is two boots
    (C)   the opportunity cost of moving from point A to point B is two hats
    (D)   the opportunity cost of moving from point A to point B is 40 hats
    (E)   the opportunity cost of moving from point A to point D is two boots

----

4. To correct for a severe inflation, what fiscal policy measure would be appropriate?

    (A)   increase the money supply
    (B)   decrease the money supply
    (C)   increase government spending
    (D)   increase taxes
    (E)   increase deficit spending

5. If real GDP grew by 6% during a period when inflation was 4%, then

    (A)   nominal GDP grew by 2%
    (B)   nominal GDP grew by 4%
    (C)   nominal GDP grew by 6%
    (D)   nominal GDP grew by 10%
    (E)   nominal GDP fell by 2%

6. Which of the following groups will benefit the most if actual inflation is less than anticipated inflation?

    (A)   banks that loaned out money with a fixed interest rate
    (B)   banks that loaned out money with a variable interest rate
    (C)   consumers who purchased homes with fixed rate mortgages
    (D)   consumers who purchased homes with a variable interest rate
    (E)   banks and consumers would benefit by the same amount

7. Which of the following people is least likely to be affected by cyclical unemployment?

    (A)   an assembly line worker in an automobile manufacturing plant
    (B)   a carpenter working on new home construction projects
    (C)   a police officer
    (D)   a travel agent
    (E)   an airline pilot

8. Which of the following events combined would result in the most expansionary effect on an economy?

	Taxes	Government Spending	Net Exports	Reserve Requirement
(A)	decrease	increase	increase	decrease
(B)	increase	increase	increase	decrease
(C)	decrease	increase	decrease	decrease
(D)	decrease	decrease	decrease	decrease
(E)	increase	decrease	decrease	increase

9. If the consumer price index (CPI) is 200 at the end of 2008, and 220 at the end of 2009, then inflation during 2009 was

   (A) 10 percent
   (B) 20 percent
   (C) 200 percent
   (D) 220 percent
   (E) 420 percent

10. If actual inflation exceeds anticipated inflation, then real wages will

   (A) rise
   (B) fall
   (C) remain unchanged
   (D) rise or fall depending on the wage rate
   (E) be as likely to rise or fall

11. If government spending increases by $100 and taxes increase by $100, which of the following combinations would correctly explain the effect on the budget and GDP?

	Budget	GDP
A	unchanged	decrease
B	deficit	decrease
C	unchanged	no change
D	surplus	increase
E	unchanged	increase

   (A) A
   (B) B
   (C) C
   (D) D
   (E) E

12. The "full-employment unemployment rate" is defined as the unemployment rate when

   (A) cyclical unemployment is zero
   (B) structural unemployment is zero
   (C) frictional unemployment is zero
   (D) seasonal unemployment is zero
   (E) all of the above are zero

Question 13 – 14 refer to the data below.

Population	200 million
Number in the labor force	180 million
Number employed	171 million
Number unemployed	9 million

13. Based on the data above, what is the labor force participation rate?

   (A) 100 percent
   (B) 90 percent
   (C) 60 percent
   (D) 20 percent
   (E) 2 percent

14. Based on the data above, what is the unemployment rate of the economy?

   (A) 80 percent
   (B) 25 percent
   (C) 10 percent
   (D) 5 percent
   (E) 4.5 percent

_____

15. Which of the following would be the correct Keynesian fiscal policy response to an inflationary episode?

   (A) increase taxes and increase federal government spending
   (B) increase taxes and decrease federal government spending
   (C) decrease taxes and decrease federal government spending
   (D) decrease taxes and increase federal government spending
   (E) decrease taxes and increase the federal deficit

16. The view that the economy is inherently unstable and therefore should be managed to avoid cyclical fluctuations is the view held by those who have a

   (A) monetarist view toward the economy
   (B) classical view toward the economy
   (C) rational expectations view of the economy
   (D) Keynesian view toward the economy
   (E) laissez-faire view toward the economy

Question 17 refers to the graph below.

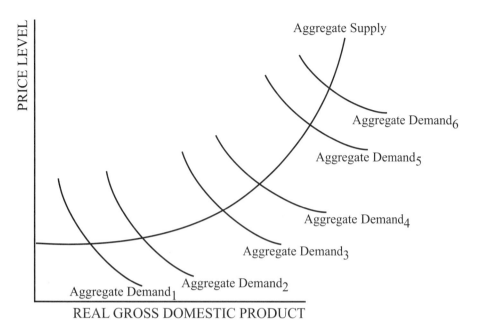

17. Based on the graph above, an increase in real output with no change in the price level would be shown by a movement from

    (A) Aggregate Demand$_1$ to Aggregate Demand$_2$
    (B) Aggregate Demand$_2$ to Aggregate Demand$_3$
    (C) Aggregate Demand$_3$ to Aggregate Demand$_4$
    (D) Aggregate Demand$_4$ to Aggregate Demand$_5$
    (E) Aggregate Demand$_5$ to Aggregate Demand$_6$

---

18. If a nation enjoys a prolonged period of mild weather and a renewed interest and aptitude toward education on the part of its youth, the likely result of these combined factors is

	GDP	Price Level
(A)	increase	increase
(B)	decrease	decrease
(C)	increase	decrease
(D)	decrease	increase
(E)	decrease	no effect

19. Which of the following would increase the size of GDP?

    I. purchasing a used textbook from the bookstore for an economics class at the local college
    II. renting a video from your local video store
    III. purchasing an antique coin set from a local store
    IV. purchasing a new memory upgrade package for an old computer

    (A) I only
    (B) II only
    (C) I and III only
    (D) II and IV only
    (E) I, II, III, and IV

20. When an economy uses more isolationist policies and engages in less free trade with other economies, we would most likely find that economy

    (A) moving closer to its production possibilities frontier
    (B) moving farther away from its production possibilities frontier
    (C) gaining more of a comparative advantage in production
    (D) gaining more of an absolute advantage in production
    (E) less likely to experience domestic inflation

21. Economic growth would be slowed the most by which of the following combination of events?

	Investment	Interest Rates	Savings Rate
A	high	high	low
B	low	low	low
C	low	high	low
D	low	low	high
E	high	high	high

    (A) A
    (B) B
    (C) C
    (D) D
    (E) E

Questions 22 – 24 refer to the graph below.

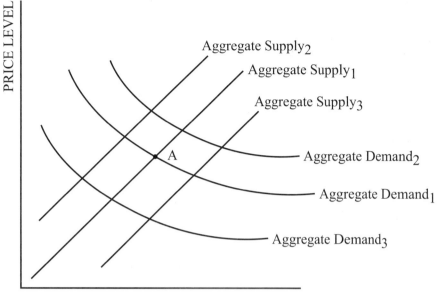

REAL GROSS DOMESTIC PRODUCT

22. Beginning at the equilibrium position shown by point A in the graph above, which single movement could cause demand-pull inflation?

(A) Aggregate Supply$_1$ to Aggregate Supply$_2$
(B) Aggregate Supply$_1$ to Aggregate Supply$_3$
(C) Aggregate Demand$_1$ to Aggregate Demand$_2$
(D) Aggregate Demand$_1$ to Aggregate Demand$_3$
(E) None of the above would explain inflation

23. Beginning at the equilibrium position shown by point A in the graph above, which single movement could demonstrate cost-push inflation?

(A) Aggregate Supply$_1$ to Aggregate Supply$_2$
(B) Aggreate Supply$_1$ to Aggregate Supply$_3$
(C) Aggregate Demand$_1$ to Aggregate Demand$_2$
(D) Aggregate Demand$_1$ to Aggregate Demand$_3$
(E) None of the above would explain inflation

24. Economic stagnation combined with inflation (stagflation) could be caused by which single shift in the graph above?

(A) Aggregate Supply$_1$ to Aggregate Supply$_2$
(B) Aggregate Supply$_1$ to Aggregate Supply$_3$
(C) Aggregate Demand$_1$ to Aggregate Demand$_2$
(D) Aggregate Demand$_1$ to Aggregate Demand$_3$
(E) Any of these has an equal chance of creating stagflation

25. Which of the following is most likely to be reduced by countercyclical fiscal and monetary policies?

    (A) seasonal unemployment
    (B) cyclical unemployment
    (C) frictional unemployment
    (D) structural unemployment
    (E) classical unemployment

26. Which of the following would be the appropriate monetary policy to reduce unemployment?

    (A) increase taxes
    (B) decrease taxes
    (C) sell bonds
    (D) buy bonds
    (E) raise the reserve requirement

27. The combined effect of contractionary fiscal policy and contractionary monetary policy would be which of the following?

	Effect on GDP	Effect on Interest Rates	Effect on the International Value of the Dollar
(A)	increase	increase	increase
(B)	decrease	decrease	increase
(C)	decrease	indeterminate	decrease
(D)	decrease	indeterminate	increase
(E)	decrease	indeterminate	indeterminate

Questions 28 – 29 refer to the graph below.

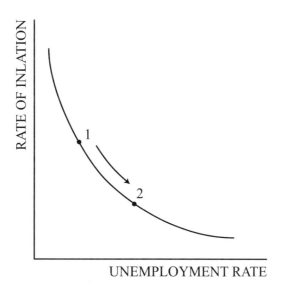

28. The graph above is a

    (A) short-run Keynesian aggregate demand curve
    (B) long-run Laffer curve
    (C) short-run Laffer curve
    (D) long-run Phillips curve
    (E) short-run Phillips curve

29. Movement from point 1 to point 2 on the graph above, could be caused by which of the following?

    (A) a leftward shift in aggregate demand
    (B) a rightward shift in aggregate demand
    (C) a leftward shift in aggregate supply
    (D) a rightward shift in aggregate supply
    (E) rightward shift in production possibilities

----

30. If an economy finds that real GDP increases by $1,000 as a result of a $100 government spending program then for that economy the marginal propensity to save must be

    (A) .10
    (B) 10
    (C) 100
    (D) 900
    (E) 1,000

31. Aggregate demand is comprised of which of the following?

   (A) Consumption expenditures + Investment expenditures + Government expenditures + Exports –
       Imports
   (B) Consumption expenditures + Investment expenditures + Government expenditures + Savings +
       Exports – Imports
   (C) Consumption expenditures + Investment expenditures + Government expenditures – Exports –
       Imports
   (D) Consumption expenditures + Investment expenditures + Government expenditures + Business
       expenditures + Savings + Exports + Imports
   (E) Consumption expenditures + Investment expenditures + Government expenditures + Exports +
       Imports

32. The ability of banks to create money in a fractional reserve banking system in countries like the United
    States is based on

   (A) individuals keeping all of their money on deposit in banks
   (B) banks keeping a fraction of customers deposits as reserves
   (C) banks keeping a fraction of central bank deposits as reserves
   (D) central banks keeping a fraction of banks deposits as reserves
   (E) central banks keeping a fraction of customer deposits as reserves

33. The way that monetary policy is transmitted through the economy is correctly described in which of
    the following?

	Money Supply	Interest Rate	Investment	GDP
(A)	increase	increase	increase	increase
(B)	increase	increase	increase	decrease
(C)	increase	decrease	increase	increase
(D)	increase	decrease	decrease	decrease
(E)	decrease	decrease	decrease	decrease

34. Falling interest rates have a tendency to promote economic growth because

   (A) the capital stock will decrease.
   (B) the capital stock will increase.
   (C) consumers will spend more.
   (D) aggregate demand will increase
   (E) money will be worth more.

35. An inflationary gap could be eliminated by

   (A) an increase in the federal governments budget deficit
   (B) an increase in the federal governments budget surplus
   (C) a decrease in the reserve requirement
   (D) a decrease in the discount rate
   (E) an increase in government spending

36. If an economy was operating at an equilibrium level of output at $7,000 billion and full-employment equilibrium was $9,000 billion, with a marginal propensity to save of .20, a Keynesian economist would recommend

    (A) increasing government spending by $2,000 billion
    (B) increasing government spending by $500 billion
    (C) decreasing taxes by $2,000 billion
    (D) decreasing taxes by $500 billion
    (E) decreasing taxes by $400 billion

37. Which of the following is most likely to occur during a period of rapidly rising GDP?

    (A) increasing unemployment rates
    (B) increasing federal budget deficits
    (C) decreasing inflationary pressure in the economy
    (D) increasing inflationary pressure in the economy
    (E) a shift in the long run Phillips curve

38. If a banking system has a reserve requirement of 10% and experiences an autonomous deposit of $1,000, which of the following is the maximum amount of money that the banks in that system could create?

    (A) $1,000
    (B) $2,000
    (C) $8,000
    (D) $9,000
    (E) $10,000

39. If the government and the Federal Reserve both attempt to contract the economy, which of the following describes the most likely results of these actions? (FP = fiscal policy, MP = monetary policy)

	Interest Rates		Price Level		Output	
	FP	MP	FP	MP	FP	MP
(A)	increase	increase	increase	increase	increase	increase
(B)	decrease	decrease	decrease	decrease	decrease	decrease
(C)	increase	decrease	increase	increase	increase	increase
(D)	decrease	increase	decrease	decrease	decrease	decrease
(E)	decrease	increase	decrease	increase	decrease	increase

40. The relationship between real interest rates and nominal interest rates is correctly described by which of the following?

    (A) real interest rate = nominal interest rate + anticipated inflation
    (B) nominal interest rate = real interest rate + anticipated inflation
    (C) real interest rate = nominal interest rate + actual inflation
    (D) nominal interest rate = real interest rate + actual inflation
    (E) nominal interest rate = real interest rate - actual inflation

41. In a circular flow diagram the interaction of businesses and households is characterized by

    I. Households buying factors of production and goods
    II. Firms buying factors of production and goods
    III. Households buying factors of production
    IV. Firms buying factors of production
    V. Firms buying goods
    VI. Households buying goods

    (A) I only
    (B) II only
    (C) III and IV only
    (D) IV and VI only
    (E) V and VI only

42. Based on the Keynesian model, which of the following would increase aggregate demand?

    (A) an increase in exports
    (B) an increase in imports
    (C) an increase in business taxes
    (D) an increase in the price level
    (E) a decrease in the price level

43. A long-run aggregate supply curve can be shifted to the right by which of the following?

    (A) an increase in aggregate demand
    (B) a decrease in aggregate demand
    (C) an increase in short-run aggregate supply
    (D) a decrease in short-run aggregate supply
    (E) a decrease in interest rates

44. Which of the following has the potential to improve conditions in an economy with a 7% annual rate of inflation and a 7% unemployment rate?

    (A) increase aggregate demand
    (B) decrease aggregate demand
    (C) increase aggregate supply
    (D) decrease aggregate supply
    (E) implement wage and price controls

Question 45 refers to the graph below.

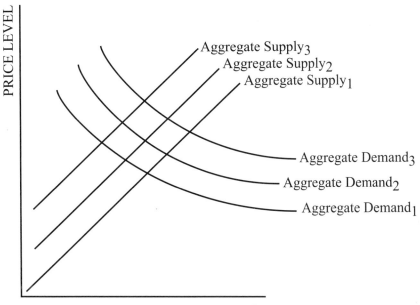

45. Which of the shifts shown in the graph above demonstrate the concept of crowding out?

    (A) Aggregate Demand$_1$ to Aggregate Demand$_2$ to Aggregate Demand$_3$
    (B) Aggregate Demand$_1$ to Aggregate Demand$_3$ to Aggregate Demand$_2$
    (C) Aggregate Supply$_1$ to Aggregate Supply$_2$ to Aggregate Supply$_3$
    (D) Aggregate Supply$_1$ to Aggregate Supply$_3$ to Aggregate Supply$_2$
    (E) Aggregate Supply$_3$ to Aggregate Supply$_2$ to Aggregate Supply$_1$

---

46. The national debt of a country would increase with which of the following?

    (A) a contractionary fiscal policy
    (B) a budget surplus for the current year
    (C) a budget deficit for the current year
    (D) a balanced budget for the current year
    (E) an expansionary monetary policy

47. If the simple spending multiplier is 5, then the

    (A) tax multiplier is also 5
    (B) marginal propensity to consume is 80%
    (C) marginal propensity to consume is 20%
    (D) savings rate is 20%
    (E) reserve requirement is 80%

48. Those who believe that modern market-based economies will achieve a desirable macroeconomic equilibrium if not tampered with

    (A) advocate the used of discretionary fiscal policy
    (B) advocate the use of discretionary monetary policy
    (C) are considered to be Keynesian in their view
    (D) are following the rational expectation view
    (E) are considered to be Classical in their view

49. An aggregate demand curve slopes down and to the right because of all of the following EXCEPT

    (A) the wealth (real balances) effect
    (B) the interest rate effect
    (C) the international effect
    (D) the price level effect
    (E) none of the above are reasons for the downward and to the right slope of the aggregate demand curve

50. If real interest rates in an economy rise, what will happen to each of the following?

	International Value of Currency	Exports	GDP	Capital Flow
(A)	increase	increase	expand	inflow
(B)	decrease	decrease	contract	outflow
(C)	increase	decrease	expand	outflow
(D)	increase	decrease	contract	inflow
(E)	decrease	increase	expand	outflow

51. If the federal government and the Federal Reserve cooperate in achieving lower real interest rates, which of the following will occur?

    (A) an increase in the capital stock and a capital inflow
    (B) an increase in the capital stock and a capital outflow
    (C) a decrease in the capital stock and a capital inflow
    (D) a decrease in the capital stock and a capital outflow
    (E) a decrease in the capital stock and no change in capital flows

52. Adverse and favorable supply shocks

    (A) can be anticipated and shift aggregate supply
    (B) can be anticipated and shift aggregate demand
    (C) cannot be anticipated and shift aggregate supply
    (D) cannot be anticipated and shift aggregate demand
    (E) can be anticipated and shift the Phillips curve

53. All of the following are included in the M1 definition of the money supply EXCEPT

  (A) coins
  (B) currency
  (C) checkable accounts
  (D) credit cards
  (E) demand deposits

54. If the Federal Reserve sells bonds, which of the following will result?

  (A) increased demand for money and lower interest rates
  (B) decreased demand for money and higher interest rates
  (C) decreased money supply and higher interest rates
  (D) increased money supply and lower interest rates
  (E) increased money supply and increased demand for money

Question 55 refers to the table below.

Output Per Unit of Labor Input

	U.S.	T.H.E.M.
Toys	10	20
Trains	20	15

55. Based on the data from the table above we can conclude that

  (A) U.S. has a comparative advantage in the production of toys and trains
  (B) T.H.E.M. has a comparative advantage in the production of toys and trains
  (C) U.S. has an absolute advantage in the production of toys and trains
  (D) T.H.E.M. has an absolute advantage in the production of toys and trains
  (E) U.S. has an absolute advantage in trains and T.H.E.M. has an absolute advantage in toys

Question 56 refers to the table below.

May	1 U.S. dollar	= 2 Fergi francs
June	1 U.S. dollar	= 3 Fergi francs

56. Based on the information in the exchange rate table above,

  (A) the U.S. dollar has become stronger and exports to Fergi will rise
  (B) the U.S. dollar has become stronger and exports to Fergi will fall
  (C) the U.S. dollar has become weaker and exports to Fergi will rise
  (D) the U.S. dollar has become weaker and exports to Fergi will fall
  (E) the U.S. dollar has become weaker but exports to Fergi will not change

Questions 57 – 58 refer to the graph below.

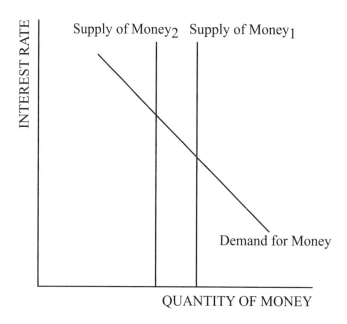

57. What is the most likely cause of the shift in the graph above?

    (A) expansionary fiscal policy
    (B) contractionary fiscal policy
    (C) expansionary monetary policy
    (D) contractionary monetary policy
    (E) wage and price controls

58. What is the most likely consequence of the shift in the graph above?

    (A) an increase in business investment spending
    (B) a decrease in business investment spending
    (C) an increase in new home construction
    (D) an increase in inflation
    (E) a decrease in unemployment

59. Which of the following best expresses the central idea of countercyclical fiscal policy?

    (A) planned deficits are experienced during economic booms and planned surpluses during economic recessions.
    (B) balanced-budgets are the proper choice for determining economic policy.
    (C) deficits are planned during economic recessions, and surpluses are utilized to restrain inflationary booms.
    (D) deficits are planned during inflationary booms, and surpluses are utilized to restrain economic recessions.
    (E) actual deficits should equal actual surpluses during a period of deflation.

60. When countries allow unrestricted international trade

   (A)   it is likely that domestic consumers could gain at the expense of some domestic producers
   (B)   it is likely that some domestic producers could gain at the expense of domestic consumers
   (C)   it is not likely for domestic consumers to gain unless domestic producers also gain
   (D)   it is not likely for domestic consumers to gain unless domestic producers lose
   (E)   there is no link between the welfare of domestic consumers or producers and international trade

Free-Response Questions

1. (a) Draw a correctly labeled aggregate supply and aggregate demand graph for an economy operating at full employment. On your graph, include each of the following:
   - (i)   a short-run aggregate supply curve
   - (II)   a long-run aggregate supply curve
   - (iii) an aggregate demand curve
   (b) Assume that the government of this economy decides to engage in a massive new road reconstruction project of rebuilding its system of interstate highways. Explain what will happen to each of the following as a result of the new project:
   - (i)   aggregate supply and aggregate demand
   - (ii)   output and the price level
   - (iii) unemployment
   (c) Suppose the government does not raise taxes to pay for this road building project but instead engages in deficit spending. Draw a correctly labeled graph of the loanable funds market to demonstrate the effect.
   (d) Based on your answer to part (c), explain what the effect on long-run economic growth will be.
   (e) Demonstrate the long-run growth effect on a correctly labeled production possibilities curve.

2. Use the information in the exchange rate table below to answer the following questions. The U.S. currency is the dollar ($). The T.H.E.M. currency is the "L":

	U.S. ($)		T.H.E.M. (L)
Day 1	1	trades for	2
Day 2	1	trades for	3

   - (a) What has happened to the value of the U.S. dollar between Day 1 and Day 2?
   - (b) What has happened to the value of the T.H.E.M. "L" between Day 1 and Day 2?
   - (c) What will happen to exports from the U.S. to T.H.E.M., on Day 2 relative to Day 1?
   - (d) What will happen to imports into the U.S. from T.H.E.M., on Day 2 relative to Day 1?
   - (e) If the change in the exchange rates were caused by a change in real interest rates in these two countries, which country must have experienced an increase in relative interest rates? Explain.

152

3. Econville has a banking system based on fractional reserves and has a central bank. The reserve requirement set by the central bank for all banks in the system is 20%. A new deposit is made into Chasey Bank of $10,000. Answer each of the following:

   (a)   What will happen to the reserves of Chasey Bank as a result of this new deposit?

   (b)   What will happen to required reserves of Chasey Bank as a result of this new deposit?

   (c)   What will happen to excess reserves of Chasey Bank as a result of this new deposit?

   (d)   Chasey Bank loans out all of its excess reserves. These are deposited into another bank in the system that in turn loans out all of its excess reserves. This process is repeated over and over until there are no more excess reserves. What will be the eventual change in the money supply of Econville that results from the initial deposit of $10,000?

   (e)   How much of the change in the money supply that you identified in part (d) was actually created by the banks in the system? Explain.

Macroeconomics

Sample Examination II

Question 1 refers to the graph below.

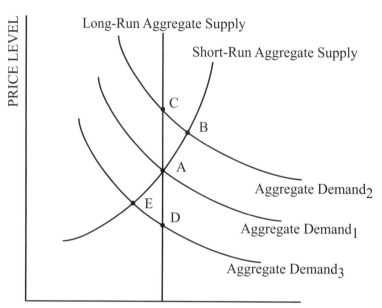

1. Assume that the United States economy has achieved long-run equilibrium at full employment. Suddenly tourist destinations in the United States become wildly popular with American and foreign citizens. If no monetary or fiscal policy actions are undertaken, which equilibrium point on the graph above will result in the long run?

   (A) A
   (B) B
   (C) C
   (D) D
   (E) E

---

2. Which of the following is the best example of structural unemployment?

   (A) a factory worker laid off because sales are slow
   (B) a landscaper who is out of work during winter
   (C) a recent college graduate has not decided which of two job offers to take
   (D) a record player repairperson who cannot find work
   (E) an assembly plant worker who is let go during a recession

154

3. Which of the following combined events would result in the most contractionary effect on an economy?

	Taxes	Government Spending	Net Exports	Reserve Requirement
(A)	decrease	increase	increase	decrease
(B)	increase	increase	increase	decrease
(C)	decrease	increase	decrease	decrease
(D)	decrease	decrease	decrease	decrease
(E)	increase	decrease	decrease	increase

4. If actual inflation equals anticipated inflation over a period for which wages were adjusted purely to account for expected inflation, then real wages will

   (A) rise
   (B) fall
   (C) remain unchanged
   (D) rise or fall depending on the wage rate
   (E) be as likely to rise or fall

Questions 5 – 6 refer to the figure below.

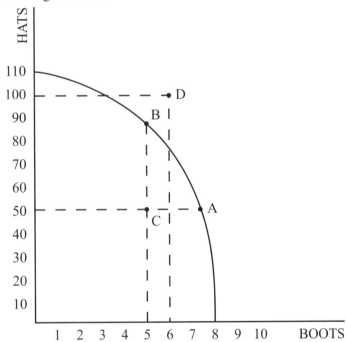

5. Which of the following statements about moving from point B to point D in the graph above, is correct?

   (A) it is not a possible point of production because the economy cannot produce as many boots as point D represents
   (B) it is not a possible point of production because the economy does not have enough resources to produce the number of hats that point D represents
   (C) it is not a possible point of production because consumer demand is not sufficient to purchase the amount of hats and boots that point D represents
   (D) it is not a possible point of production because the economy does not have enough resources to produce the number of hats and boots simultaneously that point D represents
   (E) it is a possible point of production if the economy more fully employs its resources

6. Based on the graph above, which of the following is correct?

   (A)   the opportunity cost of moving from point C to point A is two boots
   (B)   the opportunity cost of moving from point C to point A is 50 hats
   (C)   the opportunity cost of moving from point C to point A is zero
   (D)   the opportunity cost of moving from point B to point D is one hat
   (E)   the opportunity cost of moving from point B to point D is one boot

———————————

7. If a banking system has a reserve requirement of 20% and experiences an autonomous deposit of $5,000, which of the following is the maximum amount of money that the banks in that system could create?

   (A) $1,000
   (B) $5,000
   (C) $10,000
   (D) $20,000
   (E) $25,000

8. Which of the following would be the correct Keynesian fiscal policy responses to a recessionary episode?

   (A)   increase taxes and increase federal government spending
   (B)   increase taxes and decrease federal government spending
   (C)   decrease taxes and decrease federal government spending
   (D)   decrease taxes and increase federal government spending
   (E)   decrease taxes and decrease the federal deficit

9. The Keynesian view of macroeconomic stability is that most groups in society act in a pro-cyclical manner and therefore there is only one group that has the responsibility to act in a counter-cyclical manner. What is that single group?

   (A)   consumers
   (B)   the government
   (C)   business
   (D)   foreigners
   (E)   entrepreneurs

Question 10 refers to the graph below.

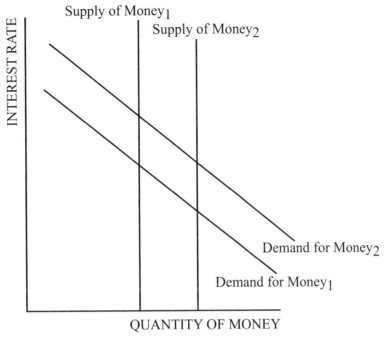

QUANTITY OF MONEY

10. Which shift shown in the graph above would be the result of expansionary monetary policy?

    (A)   Supply of Money$_1$ to Supply of Money$_2$

    (B)   Supply of Money$_2$ to Supply of Money$_1$

    (C)   Demand for Money$_1$ to Demand for Money$_2$

    (D)   Demand for Money$_2$ to Demand for Money$_1$

    (E)   Demand for Money$_1$ to Supply of Money$_1$

---

11. If the Federal Reserve buys bonds, which of the following will result?

    (A)   increased demand for money and lower interest rates

    (B)   decreased demand for money and higher interest rates

    (C)   decreased money supply and higher interest rates

    (D)   increased money supply and lower interest rates

    (E)   increased money supply and increased demand for money

12. If real interest rates in an economy fall, what will happen to each of the following?

	International Value of Currency	Exports	GDP
(A)	increase	increase	expand
(B)	decrease	decrease	contract
(C)	increase	decrease	expand
(D)	increase	decrease	contract
(E)	decrease	increase	expand

13. The national debt of a country would decrease with which of the following?

    (A) an expansionary fiscal policy
    (B) a budget surplus for the current year
    (C) a budget deficit for the current year
    (D) a balanced budget for the current year
    (E) a contractionary monetary policy

14. If the simple spending multiplier is 4, then

    (A) the tax multiplier is also 4
    (B) the marginal propensity to consume is 75%
    (C) the marginal propensity to consume is 25%
    (D) the savings rate is 25%
    (E) the reserve requirement is 25%

15. Which of the following would NOT increase real GDP?

    (A) an increase in business inventories
    (B) a retired person receiving a pension check
    (C) a consumer getting a haircut at the local barber shop
    (D) a local fire department buying a new fire truck
    (E) a foreigner purchasing a domestically made product

16. If nominal GDP grew by 6%, during a period when real GDP grew by 4%,

    (A) inflation was 10%
    (B) inflation was 6%
    (C) inflation was 4%
    (D) inflation was 2%
    (E) inflation was -2%

17. The view that monetary policy is ineffective because it can be anticipated is the

    (A) monetarist view toward the economy
    (B) classical view toward the economy
    (C) rational expectations view of the economy
    (D) Keynesian view toward the economy
    (E) laissez-faire view toward the economy

18. Economic growth would be enhanced the most by which of the following combinations of events?

	Investment	Interest Rates	Literacy Rate
A	high	high	low
B	low	low	low
C	low	high	low
D	high	low	high
E	high	high	high

(A) A
(B) B
(C) C
(D) D
(E) E

Question 19 refers to the graph below.

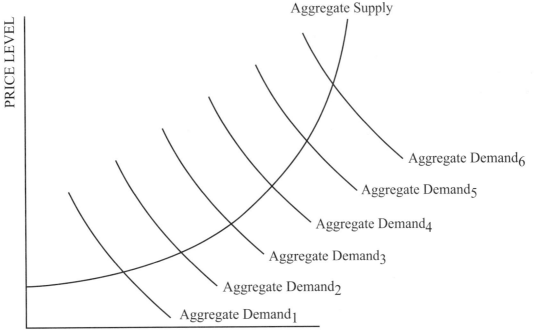

19. Based on the graph above, the increase in real output with the largest increase in the price level would be shown by a movement from

(A) Aggregate Demand$_1$ to Aggregate Demand$_2$
(B) Aggregate Demand$_2$ to Aggregate Demand$_3$
(C) Aggregate Demand$_3$ to Aggregate Demand$_4$
(D) Aggregate Demand$_4$ to Aggregate Demand$_5$
(E) Aggregate Demand$_5$ to Aggregate Demand$_6$

<u>Questions 20 – 21</u> refers to the graph below.

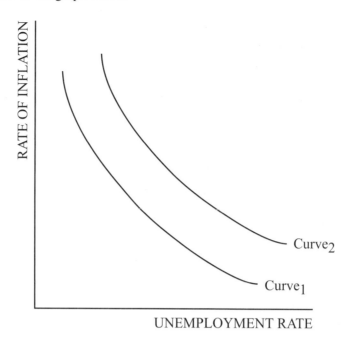

UNEMPLOYMENT RATE

20. Curve 1 in the graph above is a

(A) short run Keynesian aggregate demand curve
(B) long run Laffer curve
(C) short run Laffer curve
(D) long run Phillips curve
(E) short run Phillips curve

21. Movement from Curve 1 to Curve 2 in the graph above, could be caused by which of the following?

(A) a leftward shift in aggregate demand
(B) a rightward shift in aggregate demand
(C) a leftward shift in aggregate supply
(D) a rightward shift in aggregate supply
(E) a rightward shift in production possibilities

—————————

22. Which of the following would be the appropriate monetary policy to reduce inflation?

(A) increase taxes
(B) decrease taxes
(C) sell bonds
(D) buy bonds
(E) lower the federal funds rate

23. If a country switched from a fractional reserve banking system to a system of 100 percent reserves

    (A) the banking system would be unable to create money
    (B) the banking system would be able to create more money
    (C) the central bank would be unable to create money
    (D) the simple money multiplier would increase
    (E) the ability of the central bank to carry on monetary policy would be increased

24. Which of the following groups would benefit the most if actual inflation is greater than anticipated inflation?

    (A) banks that loaned out money with a fixed interest rate
    (B) banks that loaned out money with a variable interest rate
    (C) consumers who purchased homes with fixed rate mortgages
    (D) consumers who purchased homes with a variable interest rate
    (E) banks and consumers would benefit by the same amount

25. If government spending decreases by $500 and taxes decrease by $500, which of the following combinations would correctly explain the effect on the budget and GDP?

	Budget	GDP
A	unchanged	decrease
B	deficit	decrease
C	unchanged	no change
D	surplus	increase
E	unchanged	increase

    (A) A
    (B) B
    (C) C
    (D) D
    (E) E

Questions 26 – 28 refer to the graph below.

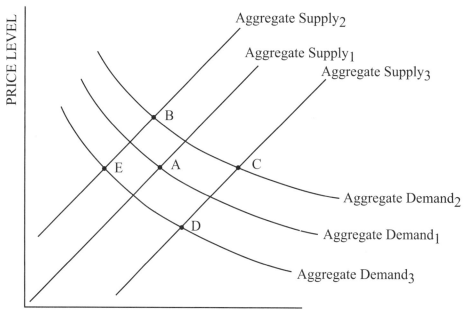

26. Beginning at the equilibrium position shown by point A in the graph above, which single movement could be caused by an increase in disposable income?

    (A)   Aggregate Supply$_1$ to Aggregate Supply$_2$
    (B)   Aggregate Supply$_1$ to Aggregate Supply$_3$
    (C)   Aggregate Demand$_1$ to Aggregate Demand$_2$
    (D)   Aggregate Demand$_1$ to Aggregate Demand$_3$
    (E)   Aggregate Demand$_3$ to Aggregate Demand$_1$

27. Beginning at the equilibrium position shown by point A in the graph above, which of the following could cause a movement to point B?

    (A)   increased technology and increased income
    (B)   decreased technology and decreased income
    (C)   increased technology and decreased income
    (D)   decreased technology and increased income
    (E)   increased government spending and increased taxes on consumers

28. An increase in real GDP with no inflation can be demonstrated by a movement from point A to which point in the graph above?

    (A)   A
    (B)   B
    (C)   C
    (D)   D
    (E)   E

29. The natural rate of unemployment is defined as the unemployment rate when

    (A) cyclical unemployment is zero
    (B) structural unemployment is zero
    (C) frictional unemployment is zero
    (D) seasonal unemployment is zero
    (E) all of the above are zero

30. A recessionary gap could be eliminated by

    (A) an increase in the federal government spending
    (B) an increase in the federal taxes
    (C) an increase in the reserve requirement
    (D) an increase in the federal funds rate
    (E) an increase in interest rates

31. To correct for a severe recession what fiscal policy measure would be appropriate?

    (A) increase the money supply
    (B) decrease the money supply
    (C) increase government spending
    (D) increase taxes
    (E) decrease deficit spending

32. When the Federal Reserve engages in open market operations they are buying and selling

    (A) corporate bonds
    (B) municipal bonds
    (C) Federal Reserve bonds
    (D) U.S. government bonds
    (E) foreign bonds

33. If an economy suddenly experiences a significant increase in income, output, and employment which of the following is least likely to increase?

    (A) consumption
    (B) investment
    (C) government revenue
    (D) exports
    (E) imports

34. A movement toward a policy of unrestricted free trade could do which of the following?

    (A) extend a nation's production possibilities frontier
    (B) contract a nation's production possibilities frontier
    (C) remove a comparative advantage in production for that nation
    (D) remove an absolute advantage in production for that nation
    (E) increase the likelihood of inflation for that nation

35. If an economy finds that real GDP increases by $400 as a result of a $100 tax cut then for that economy the marginal propensity to save must be

(A) .10
(B) .20
(C) .25
(D) .30
(E) 4

Questions 36 – 37 refer to the date below.

Population	300 million
Number in the labor force	240 million
Number employed	204 million
Number unemployed	36 million

36. Based on the data above, what is the labor force participation rate?

(A) 100 percent
(B) 85 percent
(C) 80 percent
(D) 20 percent
(E) 12 percent

37. Based on the information above, what is the unemployment rate of the economy?

(A) 85 percent
(B) 22 percent
(C) 18 percent
(D) 15 percent
(E) 12 percent

Question 38 refers to the table below.

Output Per Unit of Labor Input

	U.S.	Y.O.U.
Cars	3	2
Computers	20	5

38. Based on the data from the table above we can conclude that

(A) U.S. has a comparative advantage in the production of cars and computers
(B) Y.O.U. has a comparative advantage in the production of cars and computers
(C) U.S. has an absolute advantage in the production of cars and computers
(D) Y.O.U. has an absolute advantage in the production of cars and computers
(E) U.S. has a comparative advantage in cars and Y.O.U. has a comparative advantage in computers

---

39. The combined effect of expansionary fiscal policy and expansionary monetary policy would result in which of the following?

	Effect on GDP	Effect on Interest Rates	Effect on the International Value of the Dollar
(A)	decrease	increase	increase
(B)	increase	decrease	increase
(C)	increase	indeterminate	decrease
(D)	increase	indeterminate	increase
(E)	increase	indeterminate	indeterminate

40. Based on the information in the following exchange rate table:

October   1 U.S. dollar = 4 Fergi francs
November   1 U.S. dollar = 3 Fergi francs

(A) the U.S. dollar has become stronger and exports to Fergi will rise
(B) the U.S. dollar has become stronger and exports to Fergi will fall
(C) the U.S. dollar has become weaker and exports to Fergi will rise
(D) the U.S. dollar has become weaker and exports to Fergi will fall
(E) the U.S. dollar has become weaker but exports to Fergi will not change

41. Which of the following is most likely to occur during a prolonged period of rapidly falling GDP?

(A) a decline in unemployment rates
(B) an increase in the federal budget deficit
(C) an increase in interest rates
(D) increasing inflationary pressure in the economy
(E) a shift in the long run Phillips curve

42. If the consumer price index (CPI) were 300 at the end of 2008 and 321 at the end of 2009, then inflation during 2008 was

(A) 7 percent
(B) 21 percent
(C) 100 percent
(D) 300 percent
(E) 330 percent

43. If a nation suffers a period of adverse supply shocks, the likely result is

	GDP	Price Level
(A)	increase	increase
(B)	decrease	decrease
(C)	increase	decrease
(D)	decrease	increase
(E)	decrease	no effect

44. If the federal government engages in expansionary fiscal policy which of the following is most likely to occur?

    (A) an increase in the demand for loanable funds and an increase in interest rates
    (B) an increase in the demand for loanable funds and a decrease in interest rates
    (C) a decrease in the demand for loanable funds and a decrease in interest rates
    (D) an increase in the demand for money and a decrease in interest rates
    (E) a decrease in the demand for money and a decrease in interest rates

45. Which of the following is least likely to influence long-run economic growth?

    (A) the size of the capital stock
    (B) the size of the labor force
    (C) the unemployment rate
    (D) state of technology
    (E) interest rates

46. One way that fiscal policy is transmitted through the economy is correctly described by which of the following?

	Taxes	Disposable Income	Consumption	GDP
(A)	increase	increase	increase	increase
(B)	increase	increase	increase	decrease
(C)	increase	decrease	increase	increase
(D)	increase	decrease	decrease	decrease
(E)	decrease	decrease	decrease	decrease

47. Which of the following has the potential to cause a change in the unemployment rate from 5% to 7% and, at the same time a change in the inflation rate from 3% to 6%?

    (A) an increase in aggregate demand
    (B) a decrease in aggregate demand
    (C) an increase in aggregate supply
    (D) a decrease in aggregate supply
    (E) the implementation of wage and price controls

48. Based on the Keynesian model, which of the following would decrease aggregate demand?

    (A) a decrease in aggregate supply
    (B) a decrease in the price level
    (C) a decrease in exports
    (D) a decrease in imports
    (E) a decrease in business taxes

49. If an economy were operating at an equilibrium level of output at $6,000 billion and full employment equilibrium was $5,000 billion, with a marginal propensity to save of .25, a Keynesian economist would recommend

    (A)   decrease government spending by $1,000 billion
    (B)   increase government spending by $250 billion
    (C)   decrease government spending by $250 billion
    (D)   increase taxes by $250 billion
    (E)   decrease taxes by $250 billion

50. If real interest rates in an economy are 8% and nominal interest rates in that same economy are 10%, then the anticipated rate of inflation in that economy must be

    (A)   -2%
    (B)   2%
    (C)   8%
    (D)   10%
    (E)   18%

51. If the government and the Federal Reserve both attempt to expand the economy, which of the following describes the most likely results of these actions? (FP = fiscal policy, MP = monetary policy)

	Interest Rates		Price Level		Output	
	FP	MP	FP	MP	FP	MP
(A)	increase	increase	increase	increase	increase	increase
(B)	decrease	decrease	decrease	decrease	decrease	decrease
(C)	increase	decrease	increase	increase	increase	increase
(D)	decrease	increase	decrease	decrease	decrease	decrease
(E)	decrease	increase	decrease	increase	decrease	increase

52. If fiscal and monetary policies both result in achieving higher real interest rates which of the following will occur?

    (A)   an increase in the capital stock and a capital inflow
    (B)   an increase in the capital stock and a capital outflow
    (C)   a decrease in the capital stock and a capital inflow
    (D)   a decrease in the capital stock and a capital outflow
    (E)   a decrease in the capital stock and no change in capital flows

53. Which of the following is most likely to be avoided by countercyclical fiscal and monetary policies?

    (A)   an unemployed construction worker who is laid off due to bad weather
    (B)   an unemployed welder who was replaced by a robotic welder
    (C)   an unemployed recent college graduate trying to decide between two job offers
    (D)   an unemployed factory worker who is laid off due to slow sales
    (E)   an underemployed taxi driver who lost a job at the post office

54. A long-run aggregate supply curve can be shifted to the left by which of the following?

    (A) a decrease in aggregate demand
    (B) a decrease in short-run aggregate supply
    (C) an increase in exports
    (D) an increase in imports
    (E) an increase in interest rates

55. Fiat money, like the Federal Reserve Notes used in the United States, is valuable because it is

    (A) relatively scarce
    (B) backed by gold
    (C) an asset of the Federal Reserve
    (D) an asset of the federal government
    (E) in large demand

Question 56 refers to the graph below.

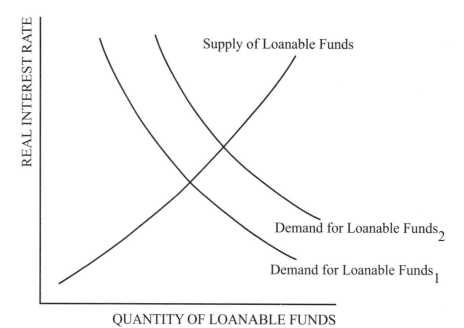

56. What is the most likely consequence of the shift in the graph above?

    (A) an increase in business investment spending
    (B) a decrease in business investment spending
    (C) an increase in new home construction
    (D) an increase in inflation
    (E) a decrease in unemployment

57. When countries follow a policy of free trade

   (A) it is possible that some domestic consumers could gain at the expense of domestic producers
   (B) it is possible that some domestic producers could gain at the expense of domestic consumers
   (C) it is impossible for domestic consumers to gain unless domestic producers also gain
   (D) it is impossible for domestic consumers to gain unless domestic producers lose
   (E) there is no link between the welfare of domestic consumers or producers and international trade

58. Which of the following would increase the size of GDP?

   I. a government purchase of a new missile delivery system
   II. a government transfer payment to a retired veteran
   III. a consumer purchase of common stock
   IV. a consumer purchase of a savings bond
   V. construction of a new home

   (A) I, only
   (B) II, only
   (C) V, only
   (D) I and V, only
   (E) I, II, III, IV, and V

59. Those who believe that economies can achieve a long-run equilibrium at any level of output, whether or not it is at potential output

   (A) do not advocate the use of discretionary fiscal policy
   (B) do not advocate only the use of discretionary monetary policy
   (C) are following a laissez-faire view
   (D) are following the Keynesian view
   (E) are considered to be Classical in their view

60. An aggregate demand curve slopes down and to the right because of

   (A) the wealth (real balances) effect
   (B) the opportunity cost effect
   (C) the multiplier effect
   (D) the price level effect
   (E) the loanable funds effect

Free-Response Questions

1. (a) Draw a correctly labeled aggregate supply and aggregate demand graph for the United States economy operating at a short-run equilibrium below full employment. On your graph include each of the following:
   (i)   a short-run aggregate supply curve
   (ii)   a long-run aggregate supply curve
   (iii)   an aggregate demand curve
   (b)   Assume that the government of the United States decides to engage fiscal policy to correct the situation described in part (a). List one fiscal policy action the government could take.
   (c)   Assume that the Federal Reserve Baml of the United States decides to engage in monetary policy to correct the situation in part (a). List two monetary policy actions the Federal Reserve could take.
   (d)   Use a correctly labeled graph to explain the effect of the fiscal policy move in part (b) on interest rates.
   (e)   Use a correctly labeled graph to explain the effect of the monetary policy move in part (c) on interest rates.
   (f)   Draw a correctly labeled short-run Phillips curve to demonstrate the effect of the fiscal policy move in part (b).

2. America suddenly becomes a popular world wide tourist destination:

   (a)   Draw a correctly labeled graph of the market for the U.S. dollar to demonstrate the effect of this new popularity with tourists.
   (b)   Explain what will happen to each of the following as a result of the increased tourist activity:
   (i)   aggregate supply and aggregate demand
   (ii)   exports
   (iii)   imports
   (iv)   capital flows

3. Economic indicators are frequently used to measure the performance of an economy like the United States:

   (a)   Unemployment is one of the economic indicators used. List three types of unemployment.
   (b)   Explain why "full employment" is not considered to be 0% unemployment.
   (c)   Inflation is another of the indicators used. Draw a correctly labeled aggregate supply and aggregate demand curve to demonstrate each of the following:
   (i)   demand-pull inflation
   (ii)   cost-push inflation
   (d)   Explain what is meant by the term "stagflation."

170